THE FUTURE ENVELOPE 1

A Multidisciplinary Approach

edited by
Ulrich Knaack & Tillmann Klein

ISBN   978-1-58603-827-4

Published and distributed by IOS Press under the imprint Delft University Press

Publisher   IOS Press BV
Nieuwe Hemweg 6b
1013 BG Amsterdam
The Netherlands

tel: +31-20-688 3355

fax: +31-20-687 0019

email: info@iospress.nl

website: www.iospress.nl
www.dupress.nl

Editors
Ulrich Knaack   uk@pduk.de
Tillmann Klein   t.klein@tudelft.nl

Layout & Bookcover Design
Ronald Visser

This publication was made at the occasion of *The Future Envelope*, a Symposium held at 11 June
2007 in Delft. This Symposium was organized by the Faculty of Architecture, Delft University of Technology (Chair Design of Construction) in cooperation with VMRG, Vereniging Metalen Ramen en
Gevelbrance.

PRINTED IN THE NETHERLANDS

PREFACE

It is a privilege to work within the innovative field of the construction industry. Especially since we probably are in the middle of what at the end will appear to have been a revolution. The contemporaries of James Watt were not aware that they were part of what we now call the industrial revolution. Only on looking back we were able to determine that the changes were quite drastic and that it merited the label of revolution. I am convinced that something like that is happening in our era. Developments in the field of a.o. industrialization, energy and climate, environment, automation and digitalisation, lack of labour, new materials, are quite significant and are forcing us to re-evaluate the field of construction as a whole. For that reason it is to be expected that during the coming decades building technology and its process will change drastically. There is thus a strong need for innovative visions about future construction.

I was invited to act as a peer reviewer for this book about the future envelope and in line with that to write this preface. Through this I am pleased to have the opportunity to contribute to the discussion on building innovation.

The starting point for the Façade Research Group are also the driving forces for development: Energy, Ecology and Efficiency. From a societal point of view I agree on the 3E mindset. One of the major tasks however is not to jump to solutions immediately but to define the targets within these areas more specifically and in a measurable way. That is not an easy job. There are a lot of stakeholders in the building industry and they probably all have their own agenda and as a result their own drives for development. It is important to define these drives carefully (with repeatable research results) as the total programme will be based on such a point of departure. Measurability is crucial in order to be able to monitor future results.

It is proven that a systematic approach increases the rate of success substantially. This implies the need for firm strategic analyses before addressing the research content. In his contribution, Wim Poelman reaffirms the necessity of a systematic approach. Here the routine of the industrial designer is contrasted with the architectural approach that is mostly based on rational and irrational considerations on a project level. The façade industry may be one of the most advanced disciplines in the building industry. Still the percentage of buildings with progressive, innovative facades is in the minority. According to Rogers' diffusion theory, modern facades are still only for the innovators and early adaptors. It is often stated that the building industry is conservative. There are many explanations for this phenomenon. The complexity of the supply chain with fragmented interests is one of them. Broadly accepted change therefore will not come rapidly. We can expect our revolution to range over the next few decades. Still, from year to year we will increasingly come across visible milestones.

It is understandable that in a technical university the focus is on technology, but one should keep in mind that technology cannot be separated from a broader vision. We need a cohesive picture and some research effort, perhaps in cooperation with some non technical universities, is of relevance. The majority of innovation achieved will consist of new products. However, design tools and new approaches to process will explicitly have to be part of the progress to be made. Tools can for example help to benefit of new technology visibly. This is about creating values. For example soundly based productivity figures for building users could stimulate the application of advanced façade technology drastically. It would be a fantastic driver to have reliable tools and models to convince commissioners on this point. Perhaps this may even turn out to be an even greater act of innovation in terms of change than façade development itself. It is however interesting to bring the facade in relation to the building concept and the utility question as a whole. In such a context volume reduction (lean walls and partitions) could be an interesting example of creating value as the user has substantially more space at his disposal within the same gross measures of the building.

An important process issue and part of my own research programme (Slimbouwen) is the organisation of the industrial process which is much more than just about producing parts with industrial technology. The research on an industrial building process focuses on creating a situation in which contractors on building sites are able to work without interweaving with other disciplines. In relation to facades the question for example is how to deal with services. Integrated with connecting leads for connection with the infrastructure (the façade as a machine) or disintegrated with accessible hollow spaces in the elements. The industrial approach will most certainly lead to other forms of project organisation including the design and preparation phase as well as, for example, new technologies for joints facilitating the industrial process.

A resetting of the building process as a whole is unavoidable. We just cannot go on with solving problems on an ad hoc basis. As a result of the fragmented supply chain we have been innovating incrementally on step by step basis on a component level. It is as Michiel Cohen in his contribution says that we are solving problems and at the same time introducing new ones. The result of this is that the regular building process has meanwhile developed into quite a chaotic, inadequate and highly inefficient process in which disciplines are very much interwoven with each other.

A major part of the content of the book is directed towards solutions and original ideas. It could be considered as technology driven input. That is a very good thing to do in order to inspire and challenge the market and also to be able to have discussions on the basis of concrete material. A.o the frozen textile and sandwich structures in the aviation industry are interesting topics and relevant to the building industry. Weight and volume reduction are very relevant drivers for innovation in relation to cost control and sustainability. Ultra light (and rigid) structures are however very bad preconditions for achieving a sufficient sound insulation. A deeper understanding of acoustical behaviour might create openings for this technology.

Technology can be very inspiring. It is however good that the book also focuses on non technological topics. I would like to take the opportunity to call attention to items such as issues of strategy and the analysis of customer desires and demands. The customer should become more visible in the building market. Anyway, new business approaches will no doubt form another basis for future developments. It would be interesting to make an extensive inventory of possible future business models in order to feed the strategies for developing new facades. The drivers for innovation are also not all of a rational nature. In the contribution of Luke Lowings it becomes clear that also emotional, symbolic and perceptual values become important, and are perhaps underestimated drivers for development.

I hope that you the reader will feel challenged to join the creativity or to evaluate your own ideas about the future in order to keep the discussion alive. Every contribution is of relevance as long as it sincerely supports future development. Universities have, of course, a special mission to take the lead in developing long term visions and future scenarios in order to create a fecund soil for breakthroughs for the benefit of the entire building industry. This book is an inspiring example of just that.

Prof. Dr. Jos Lichtenberg
Eindhoven University of Technology
Faculty of Architecture Building and Planning
Chair Product Development

CONTENTS

Prof. Dr. Ulrich Knaack is head of the Chair Design of Construction at the Factulty of Architecture, TU Delft. In 2005 he founded the Façade Research Group and is initiator of the conference 'The Future Envelope'.

The Future Envelope 1 – A Multidisciplinary Approach. U. Knaack and T. Klein (Eds.). IOS Press, 2008.

THE FUTURE ENVELOPE

Ulrich Knaack

Design of Construction
Faculty of Architecture Delft
University of Technology

Abstract

Research in the field of façade technology has to be orientated on the current topics energy, ecology and efficiency as key items for demands on the design. Existing façade technology, after 60 years of curtain walls and 30 years of element façades, lacks new impulses and strategies for ground breaking developments. As a result, the "Façade Research Group" at the Faculty of Architecture / TU Delft has been developed and established with a focus on problem-orientated research solutions, experimental projects, planning tools, possibilities of technology transfer and future and innovative developments.

Keywords: integrated design, façade design, façade technology, façade research group, international façade master.

1.   Introduction

"The Future Envelope" – what a title and what a promise! Can we really and realistically develop the vision and future of the entire building industry – of course, we cannot! However, as a university, we have to propose opportunities for development. And what we can do is to ask – to identify what the driving forces behind the developments will be. Besides the more marketing related aspects of "fashion and interests", the most important driving force for future building development and façades will be energy: its accessibility, production and consumption. The reasons are obvious - but the important question is in how far the architectural design, the building structure and the façade need to be geared toward this development. Secondly, ecology related to environmental impact will gain even higher importance than it has today. Architecture and façade technology already deal with climate as a design tool, and ecological and energetic concepts for the design proposal are becoming the norm. However, aspects such as the energy used to produce constructional materials, the disassembly possibilities of buildings as well as the possibilities of energy production within façades need to be further investigated and implemented into the design process. Finally, efficiency will be another important topic for the planning process if the design should remain attractive throughout its lifespan - not only related to limitations of energy consumption or financial savings; but rather as a concept for efficient design solutions in terms of organisation, synergies between functions and capacity for individuality.

Now, if we define the topics energy, ecology and efficiency as key items for demands on facade design, how can we apply values to them? Energy savings alone with better insulation values or new and more efficient technical units can be considered solutions for some demands. The added value could be reusing components such as facades or even entire buildings with different, not yet known functions. Today, a building's useful lifespan is considered to be a minimum of 20 years; but this could be extended to 100 years or more – if, for example, we would configure the façade with a degree of flexibility for different uses and demands. Here we would add a value, which is not noticeable immediately, but guarantees a benefit for society and the client. Additionally, strategies for the implementation of new materials and production technology developments should be considered. The current trends of materials-oriented and surface-oriented architectural design should be a particular point of interest and attraction. Finally, the reuse of existing buildings is a topic for consideration: 60% of future building budgets will be used in the field of refurbishment and renovation, only the remaining 40% will be invested in new constructions.

Of course, architects are always interested in new technologies – they provide new topics to draw attention to the designs and new impulses for certain developments. At the same time, the building industry is conservative in principle. The reasons are various – but some of the aspects are, that on the one hand established methods of constructions exist that builders and users are used to and feel comfortable with. On the other hand, the building itself has to stay and function for a certain period of time and is mostly an individual development. Focusing on the façade, it should be noted that the façade industry as part of the building industry is – when it comes to high technology facades - one of the most advanced disciplines; it uses industrialised production processes for serial production of profiles and pre-assembled elements – but it still has to cooperate with the less developed parts of the construction process.

To extend on the above-mentioned aspects and to develop ideas for the next steps, it seems reasonable to ask what the future expectations on additional values will be. Here begins the interesting part of the assumption: do we expect more comfort, more space or more quality? Will individualization and personalisation be a future requirement or are we going to focus on the quality of space and aesthetic design?

2

2. Current Façade Technology

The façade technology of the 20th century is related to the development of the dissolution of the massive wall: the search for more structural slenderness and greater transparency resulted in the 20th century product "curtain wall". Current façades are based on post-and-rail systems - established as a construction method more than 60 years ago and related to craftsmen's oriented building technology. In addition to this, the element system, which provided first possibilities of industrialized production, has been established over more than 30 years.

With growing consciousness for the relation between façades and energy-consumption in the beginning of the 21st century, research aimed on the integration of climate-technology into the façade. This resulted in the development of double façades. Current technology can be divided into four different principles of multi-leafed façades: boxed windows, adding a signal glazed window in front of an inner window; a second skin façade where the extra layer of glass covers the entire façade; corridor facades with a glazed corridor with vertical slots in front of the inner façade; and the integration of a story-spanning chimney in the façade cavity (1, 2).

The latest developments move in two directions: the so called "hybrid façade"(3) - a combination of standard facades with fixed sun screens and boxed windows and the integration of services units in the facades –, and the "component façade", in which the integration of all building services components is established, starting with mechanical ventilation and conditioning and ending with artificial light (4).

Figure 1
Stadttor Düsseldorf / Düsseldorf - one of the early corridor facades with a timber façade as an inner layer and single glass units as external layer

Figure 2
ARAG Tower / Düsseldorf – a
combination of a story-spanning
chimney in the façade cavity and
boxed window units to provide
individual ventilation possibility

Figure 3
debitel Headquarter / Stuttgart – a
combination of an boxed façade
unit with a single layered façade,
the so called "hybrid façade"

Reviewing these developments, we can assume that the expected development steps will be highly advanced compared to existing technologies but, at the same time, are not very promising in terms of ground breaking and influential developments: the main routes are established and knowledge can only be extended by small steps because of the already existing depth. By continuing the path of adding extra layers for each additional technical function, only a limited number of further technical developments can be expected. On the other side, an export and technically oriented society such as Europe and especially the Netherlands and Germany needs fundamental research and development to maintain technical leadership. Simultaneously, a new generation of researches, planners and manufactures, able to control newly developed techniques and to integrate them into façade design is in the starting blocks. Thus, this situation bears the opportunity for a sophisticated upgrade of an entire industry.

Figure 4
Post tower Bonn – one of the first facades, were service units and double leafed facades are combined into a decentralized "component façade"

5

3. Developing a Façade Research Group

One research topic of the department of Building Technology within the Faculty of Architecture at the TU Delft is called Industrial Building: it focuses on the design/engineering-orientated, strategic and technical possibilities of industrialization in the building industry. In this context, we investigate developments in design, planning tools, computation, mass customization and new material technologies, which provide possibilities to develop future technologies, principles and systems. Therefore, the mission of the program is to develop and improve process oriented instruments such as design principles and methodologies and result oriented solutions for technologies, production processes as well as 1:1 mockups for industrialized building processes, methods, systems and products.

Figure 5
Overview of the research activities of Building Technology at the Faculty of Architecture / TU Delft

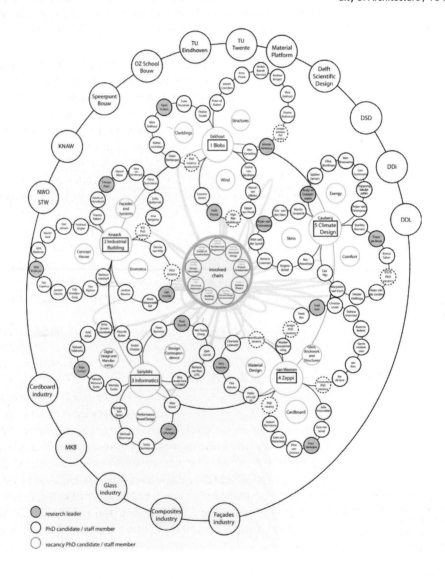

The program itself is divided into three subprograms: Facades, Concept House and Domotics – the latter two are strongly interrelated and directed towards Industrial Design Engineering.

The "Façade Research Group" was established in 2005 and focuses specifically on problem-orientated research solutions, experimental projects with a large degree of innovative technology and materials use, planning tools, possibilities of technology transfer and future and innovative developments. This group is lead by Tillman Klein.

In the area of problem oriented solutions, research in the field of free-formed cladding and the integration of these components into the planning and production process is established and executed by PhD Daan Rietbergen. Another large and promising research field, considering strategic, technical and financial parameters, is façade refurbishment, which is developed by PhD Thiemo Ebbert.

More connectional and strategically oriented are the other topic Tillmann Klein covers – technology transfer and the possibilities of these technologies in the façade industry - and Marcel Bilow's "International Façade", a planning tool for different climate zones and façade functions, to provide planners with early decision making tools fore their planning processes.

To fulfill the idea of encompassing research, topics with a large prognostic focus are also established within the group: the integral envelope – developed by Lidia Badarnah – is oriented on biological processes and technologies and shall provide the future façade with currently needed or future functions. In addition, several research projects in the field of deflateables – vacuum controlled and stabilized structures - with environment related capacities are examined by the researchers Ari Bergsma, Tillman Klein and Marcel Bilow.

Finally, the topic "Future Façade Principles" was established: organized by the author, this topic utilizes the heuristic research method of suggesting possible developments for the future, evaluating possible technical solutions and combining different disciplines and technologies - and combining these components to establish routes of developments that might not yet have been identified. The result is a collection of possibilities and opportunities – they are public, to be published and to be used by others. They are a technological offer to designers. In this context, the interest of the group is to increase the possibilities and not to keep ideas stored away, because that would mean that they would not be used and would not produce added value. The result will be a growing amount of ideas for facades or skin structures, principles or even methods of thinking.

All these activities are linked to an international network of research-ers and industries.

4.   Establishing an international network for research and education - the International Façade Master Program

To link research to practice and education, two routes of collabora-tion are established: this symposium is organised in collaboration with the VMRG – the Dutch Façade builders association – to net-work with the producing industry and its demands and possibilities.

Simultaneously, several major research projects are developed and started with Dutch and internationally operating façade industries in the field of innovative and strategic façade technologies – relat-ed to a national and international operating network of façade in Eu-rope and North America.

To provide feedback into education, an "International Facades Mas-ter" program was developed as part of the existing master pro-gram Building Technologies, starting in September 2007. The pro-gram, educating the future façade consultancies and planners for the Dutch building industry, is related to a parallel program at the "Detmold Schule für Architektur und Innenarchitektur" in Germany, with which a systematic educational exchange of students and do-cents has been established. The next step will be a link to develop-ing programs at an English University.

Figure 6
Air-B-Wall – a student project with a combination of pneumatic and vacuum constructions for deflateable and changeable façade constructions

As part of the education, a publication by Ulrich Knaack, Tillmann Klein, Marcel Bilow and Thomas Auer in collaboration with the Birkhäuser Verlag / Basel - Boston – Berlin, "Principles of Construc-tion – Façades" was published in August 2007.

5.   The Future Envelope

According to the idea of "research driven design" and "design driven research", the goal in facade research has to be to develop planning methodologies, elements and components, integration aspects, surface and climate qualities to identify the demands for energy, ecology and efficiency as key items for the design and development. In this context, the façade itself is not merely a protective surface; it acts as a part of the building, controlling climate and energy consumption and gives a surface to the building – the future envelope.

Understanding façades – or better envelopes - as part of an integral building, we have to see the task to create the future envelope on a "network" basis: systems - but also methods of thinking - which provide the possibility to develop different aspects simultaneously and combine them, as required. The envelope has to be seen as a functional part of the entire building, serving parts of the demands by providing the needed technologies and qualities. Here, we even have to withdraw from material and structure-orientated thinking and construction – we have to develop the envelope as a hybrid: materials, technologies and production processes have to be integrated in the summation and combined to an all solving result.

What a glorious request and what a promise! How can we provide the solutions and solve the problems? Of course, it is not possible to develop the answers within a secluded and isolated community – therefore, we believe in the multidisciplinary approach and the vision of this symposium: "The Future Façade" asks for ideas, wishes and visions from architects, planners, façade specialists and – very important for expanding the borders of knowledge – additional disciplines, which are not always directly related to architecture and façades.

References:

(1) T. Ebbert, U. Knaack: "The integral envelope applied for sustainable office refurbishment" 2nd CIB International Conference on Smart and Sustainable Build Environment SASBE2006

(2) A. Brookes – Cladding of Buildings – 1998

(3) Herzog, Knippers, Lang – Facade manual – 2004

(4) U. Pottgiesser – Fassadenbeschichtungen Glas – 2004

(5) Oesterle, Heussler, Lutz, Lieb – Doppelschalige Fassaden – 1999

(6) G. Hausladen – Clima Design – 2005

(7) Eekhout, Renckens – Lest best, façade conference TU Delft – 2005

(8) Bert van der Linde: De Toekomst en de Gevel, Gevelbouw 3/2007

The façade industry is an important stakeholder in the development of the future facade. Every facade design will finally pass by the industry for final execution. The façade industry is the origin for many new developments, always eager to bring it to a certain level of standardization in order to make it accessible for a broader market.

Ing. Bert Lieverse, Director of VMRG –Verenigung Metalen Ramen en Grevelbranche, underlines the potential for innovation and concentrates on strategies for the future development of the industry through growth and integration.

The Future Envelope 1 – A Multidisciplinary Approach. U. Knaack and T. Klein (Eds.). IOS Press, 2008.

DIFFERENT FUTURES

Bert Lieverse

VMRG

First, I would like to thank you for the invitation. I feel honoured to have been asked to make a presentation to such an excellent group of experts from the façade industry.

My aim for today is to give you a handle, so that you can look at your company, the market and yourself in a new way. Of course, it is up to you to do something with the information I will be giving you. Besides that, I will show you what you can see and experience through this way of looking at things, through these glasses. We will see that trends, patterns, and building blocks are there for the taking, to build our vision of the future.

1.   Looking at things from a different perspective

Why should you look at things differently? People often look at the things that are near them very intensely. We look at our specialities, our professions, and the things that go best with them. We create our own type of reality as it were, one that is different from the actual or complete reality. Different people, companies and even entire countries demonstrate this type of behaviour. If your work fascinates you, you tend to be very focused on it and get better and better at it. But only and specifically in that particular section of your field that you yourself have established and carefully keep intact. By looking at things from a different perspective, you can learn a lot of new things and that way, help to make your company more successful. I would like to make a few suggestions to help you to break free for a while from your trusted way of thinking.

2.   Respect the differences

When Toyota's Chief Executive received the award for the most successful company in Europe recently, he let it be seen that he looks at things from a different perspective than just that of a car manufacturer. He said that he believed he understood what it is that makes our interesting Europe a unity. He saw that all around Europe people were drinking beer, playing football, and serving coffee. He visited several countries in Europe and eventually found the ultimate sense of unity in the United Kingdom. But the beer was warmer there, and the football faster than in the rest of Europe and above all, the coffee turned out to be tea.

He found that Europe was a unity of differences, and that it enriched itself with those differences. All efforts to turn it into a homogeneous unity would be at the expense of the dynamic character of this important market. His message therefore was: be proud of the individual differences between people, companies, markets and countries, and then adapt your behaviour accordingly.

For Toyota this means:
- respect the uniqueness of every customer,
- respect the uniqueness of every one of the 20,000 colleagues, and
- respect all dimensions and variations of top quality.

A successful company therefore always thinks in terms of differences and does not try to force the market, the products or the customers into uniformity. This also has consequences for the internal management of a company, where your own procedures and uniform ways of working might be hostile. It is for you to be open, receptive, and to take a critical look at the vision and ways of working of your companies and ask yourself how it all fits the larger picture, the market, the industry, society and the future. On top of that, I feel that everyone – and not only the management of a company – should have an opinion about these matters.

From my position as trendwatcher, manager, trainer and policymaker in and around the façade construction industry, I certainly see the differences as well and I share the Toyota executive's opinion. It is also true for façade construction that respect for differences presents our industry with great challenges. Because this industry, too, must respect the uniqueness of every customer, every one of the 20,000 colleagues and all dimensions and variations of top quality. In my opinion, our industry adopts an all too modest position, and it deserves to play a more dominant role in construction processes.

3.   'OP DE STEP'

Since you are in Belgium, there obviously is no getting around learning a few Belgian words. I will lend you a hand. OP = ON , DE =THE en STEP= SCOOTER. I have brought one with me to show you what a modern kick scooter looks like.

We will be using the letters forming OP DE STEP to organise our thoughts and vision.

O stands for **developments in the field of Organisations**. The consequence of thinking and working with respect for differences is that organisations should no longer be regarded as structures, but as elastic work forms. Companies will continuously have to structure their organisations in a flexible manner. This means that management will be given a new role, namely that of organisation architect. In façade construction, the system suppliers and major industrial suppliers have a dominant role in Europe. This is partly due to their compulsive pursuit of uniformity. And I think that this power can be challenged if façade constructors were more flexible. It is like an octopus that has to use all its tentacles to penetrate organisations such as architects, suppliers, end users and the financiers, and that has to seek co-operation with these parties.

P stands for developments in the field of **Psychology**. It appears to be increasingly important to bind modern workers, who have become very rare, to your company. By these we mean you, your colleagues, and your work friends. It's also about motivation and personal development in your work and your profession. It is also evident that psychological knowledge makes it easier to understand what drives the people you do business with and to understand their behaviour. Especially in façade construction, where technique and technology prevail, it is important to use the insights of psychology. All the more because what makes employees so valuable is no longer physical strength but their intellectual capacities, such as knowledge and the ability to handle information. Learning processes are very much psychologically-based processes in which nothing can be forced, but that require you to find other ways of achieving success.

D stands for **Demography**. It is important to have insight into the way in which societies develop in terms of composition. Trends in society are also of importance to façade construction. The increase in the need for care and protection, such as safety, creates new demands and new possibilities for our industry. We think in terms of groups instead of countries, and therefore it is easier to trace and answer to group needs than to the needs of entire nations. You could say that there are subnations that run right across the regular country borders, with separate need patterns and characteristics. Safety, for example, is one of those cross-border phenomena that can have a different identity in different subnations. Another example is a subnation of seniors who wish for separate forms of society. Europe is shrinking and other communities are expanding. Fifty-five million Chinese live outside of China and generate a larger national product than the 1.2 billion people who live in China. The 20 million Indians outside of India represent a wealth of 340 billion dollars. Now that is food for thought…

E stands for **Economy**. Basically, the same applies here as for demography, namely that traditional country borders are no longer the determining factor. Europe is witnessing an ongoing process of unification, while major changes are taking place on a global scale. The absolute, economic supremacy of the United States is expected to make way for a new economic centre of gravity formed by the so called BRIC-countries: Brazil, Russia, India and China, together with the US and Japan. What will Europe do then? Will it become a sleeping continent or a dynamic experimental garden for technical and cultural success?

S stands for the **Social aspect**. This is about feeling, knowledge and the ability to deal with society. And that does not only apply to the corporate community, but also to the larger context spanning other companies and entire communities. It is about teamwork, about understanding decision-making processes within and between social organisations, such as companies and markets. Because it is the markets in particular that function on the basis of the social aspect. It is not only about supply and demand as an economic given, but also about creating markets and introducing products and services, including those of façade construction. It is about understanding the developments in society and the cultural aspect, for instance. And don't forget corporate culture!

T stands for **Technology**. There is a strong focus on our technology. You will understand that I consider this to be far broader than just the deepest and technologically advanced options. But even so, it is technology in particular that is one of the keys to success and an opportunity for survival in the future. Technology has caused a lot of pollution, but is can and must provide solutions. I think that there are some extraordinary challenges for façade construction here. Why do we ask fitters what energy saving entails while these people make their living out of building elaborate installations? Isn't there a smarter way of doing that? I think that in façade construction, too, creative and intelligent innovations will lead to an indispensable and ultimate success level for the 'façade' or rather 'comfort' industry. Anchoring all this in cross-border standards and regulations is one way for the industry to consolidate and expand its abilities. Active efforts on the part of the comfort industry are necessary to achieve this.

E stands for **Ecology**. Gradually the limits of our natural resources are becoming visible. It would be a good thing if the façade industry, which I will from now on refer to as the comfort industry, were to set itself up as a supplier of the solution in this respect. Energy is key here – energy control as well as energy generation. So it is not only about insulation, but also about transport, storage and the actual

14

acquiring of several forms of energy. All transport requires energy and so does all dynamics in and around work. Let the comfort industry put forward solutions on a grand scale with regard to places and environments in which to work, care, rest, play sports and live.

And finally, **P** stands for **Politics**. This mechanism, which has proven to be rather unpredictable, is a key factor determining the behaviour and the potential of national and international society. And it is in politics that the limits and the potential of the factors mentioned earlier are determined. The comfort industry will have to manifest itself on a national and international scale in order to gain and retain the dominant position it could hold.

All in all, things are becoming more complex, but also more challenging. Respecting and managing differences is what it is about, in all those fields. This applies not only to the entrepreneur or the board of directors of a company but to everybody who has a connection with what used to be referred to as the façade industry and what is now referred to as the comfort industry.

In summary:
1. Show respect and think in terms of differences.
2. Do not create strict borders but be flexible.
3. Base your activities on modern, intellectual people and focus on creativity and knowledge. Europe will be the well from which the entire comfort industry can drink. Practice continuous research and development. Innovate with creativity.
4. Create and define groups that are of importance for your company or industry yourself. Create needs and hence, markets; employ market push strategies instead of market pull strategies.
5. Orientate towards changing economic balances, or preferably dynamics on a global scale.
6. Respect and learn to deal with our wealth of different cultures.
7. Leave the façade industry and embrace comfort technology.
8. Contribute to the survival issues of nature.
9. Think in terms of policy and act politically.

More information can be found on:
www.creatiekracht.com

Prof. ir. Adriaan Beukers is a specialist for lightweight construction and composite technology in the field of aerospace engineering. The construction of airplane fuselages can be compared to that of building envelopes, although there a significant differences. Security issues are of major importance, since the failure of any part can result in a total loss. Also, airplanes are usually manufactured in larger quantities, and the financial capacities of the parties involved are bigger than in the building industry. These are some of the reasons for the aerospace industry's drive toward technology advancements.

The article was previously published in the Aeronautical Journal, Volume 107, Number 1072 in June 2003 and was specifically chosen for this book, because it explains how the philosophy of function integration can be a driving factor in the design of technical products.

* Previously published in: Aeronautical Journal, Volume 107, Number 1072, June 2003
© Aeronautical Journal. All rights reserved. Reprinted with kind permission of the Aeronautical Journal.

The Future Envelope 1 – A Multidisciplinary Approach. U. Knaack and T. Klein (Eds.). IOS Press, 2008.

AIRCRAFT STRUCTURES IN THE CENTURY AHEAD[*]

From Arts To Science, From Craftsmanship To Multidisciplinary Design And Engineering

A. Beukers,
M. van Tooren
C. Vermeeren

Faculty of Aerospace
Engineering
Delft University of Technology

Figure 1
Wright brothers

1.   Introduction

The first centennial of man's first powered flight, which was performed by Wilbur (1867-1912) and Orville (1871-1948) Wright (Fig. 1) will be celebrated in 2003. These brothers' unique and trend-setting enterprise, their skills to develop, build and commercialise controllable and load-carrying flying machines, formed the first example of a private interdisciplinary aerospace development and design initiative. It was at the same time a rare example of entrepreneurial engineering. Their work involved wind-tunnel testing of lifting devices and full-scale tests of major structural components.

Equally if not more importantly they developed an essential propulsion system consisting of a lightweight 36hp engine with four cylinders in line and a fuel injected carburettor. This engine propelled two pusher propellers through a drive system of chains. Moreover they developed the systems to control their flight. The twistable wing tips that control rolling and heading during the flight were the last remains of the former trend to mimic bird flight.

Their conceptual thinking and approach to the design and development of independent sub-components and systems, earlier advocated by Sir George Cayley (1773-1857), was in fact trend-setting. It was the start of a worldwide development of materials, aircraft concepts, engines, systems and equipment, followed and supported by design rules and tools.

Over the next 30 years most building blocks were developed to design and build reliable aircraft. It was the overture to the true revolution of industrially produced, all-aluminium, stressed skin aircraft such as the Boeing 247 (1932) and the highly successful Douglas DC-2 and DC-3 (1933). The ability to build airtight pressurised cabin structures, such as the Boeing 307 Stratoliner (1937), was the start of 70 years of evolution into the very efficient and high velocity transport system, using almost the same aircraft configurations, scaled from small to mega and equipped with very reliable high bypass jet engines[1].

---

[1] It was striking that the Wright Cyclone turbocharged nine and 18-cylinder radial piston engines played such a crucial role in that initial era. In the 1950s this engine concept was superseded by the much more reliable and efficient turbo jet engine.

Today, the aluminium aircraft concept and its manufacturing infrastructure are reaching the end of their technological possibilities. Fortunately, sciences in aeronautics and lightweight structure engineering are at the brink of the next revolution: the change from all-metal technologies to hybrid structure technologies, based on textile-reinforced polymers that are locally 'blended' with metals. In the near future a tremendous leap in materials' morphologies will take place: from intermediates such as solid plates and slender beams that are assembled and jointed mechanically, to flexible bundles of fibres (yarns) which are materialised into integral three-dimensional structures through novel textile manufacturing techniques. These textile structures are finally 'frozen'[2] or 'solidified' into ultra modern integral multipart and multifunctional solid lightweight structures.

2   The word 'frozen' is used in this essay as a metaphor for the controlled polymerisation or solidification of polymeric media (thermosetting and thermoplastic).

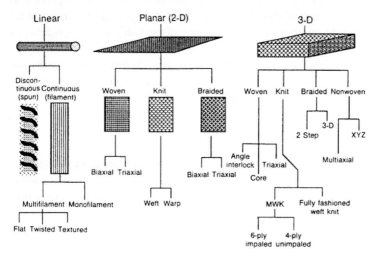

Figure 2
Classification of fibre architecture

2.   Future Aircraft Structures, A Possible Scenario

2.1   Scenario/Introduction

The authors do not intend to predict the future. The scenario presented here is rather an alternative story, a possible scenario of how aircraft structures may develop in the future. It is based on credible, relevant and challenging developments of materials, structures, transport systems and fuel technologies, not limited by today's traditions and present economic reality. By evaluating the forces that could transform new aircraft materials and structural concepts into a next generation of aircraft, and vice versa, new morphologies of aircraft materials and structures will be presented and discussed. The ways in which we provide and use aircraft in the future depends on, or is bound by, fundamental issues like:

Will the number of people with access to high velocity commercial air transport grow one-to-one with growing global prosperity or will this have to become an exclusive right for just a few of us or just for a few of our transport needs?

Can air transport meet the expanding and shifting needs for mobility of a growing urbanised world?

Can pollution by air transport, which damages health, blights environments and threatens vital natural systems, be limited?

2.2   Scenario / Energy carriers

A very important 'external' parameter for the development of new and more efficient aircraft configurations is the worlds' general future demand for new energy technologies, based on gases, Table 1. Several energy system innovations[3], beginning with the introduction of steam engines in the nineteenth century, have shown a fundamental change in dominant energy source from solid fuels to liquid ones, and in the near future to gases, natural gas CH_4 and hydrogen H_2. It is striking that the principal driving force for energy innovations, which we could regard as discontinuities in energy technologies, is not the availability of fuel, but is a market pull effect caused

[3] Energy system is fuel source plus the energy transformer (like coal, steam engine electric dynamo).

Table 1
Discontinuities in energy technologies in relation to types of transport and construction materials

Period	Energy carrier/transformer		Transport system	Materials
Up to 1830	Direct	Wood, wind, water, animals, man	Walking, horses, barges, coaches	Wood, linen, copper, brass and iron
1830-1900	Coal	Steam engines	Coaches, ships, trains	Wood, linen, iron, steel
1900-1940	Coal	Electric dynamo	Trains, cars, buses	Wood, linen, plywood, iron, steel
1903-2003	Oil	Internal combustion engines, piston and turbine engines	Cars, buses, flying machines, All aluminium aircraft with pressurised fuselages	Wood, plywood, linen, iron, steel, aluminium, polymers
1960-2025?	Oil	High efficiency by-pass turbine engines	Supersonic aircraft	Iron, steel, aluminium, polymers, titanium, composites
1970-1990	Nuclear	Centralised electricity distribution	High velocity trains	Steel, aluminium, composites
1990-2025?	Gas	Clean and efficient energy supply, CH_4 and H_2	City transport	Steel, aluminium, titanium, advanced composites, advanced alloys, ceramics
2025-future?	Hydrogen?	Fuel cell? Gas? Bio-fuels?	Sustainable transport: Smart cars and buses New aircraft and train concepts	new polymers, ceramics, fibres, new reinforcing materials and improved metals.
	Nuclear? Solar?	Direct electricity Direct electricity	high velocity train	

by end-use equipment developments, making new superior services possible (Watts, 2001). Future discontinuities in energy source exploitation could seriously affect future aircraft configuration. If hydrogen-based fuel cells would cause a transition in powered road transport for reasons of improved performance, efficiency or even sustainability, and not because of the scarcity of cheap oil, then the marketing of oil would nevertheless decline. This could seriously influence the availability and cost of liquid fuels for air transport in a negative way.

A possible future discontinuity in energy technology is the leap from liquid fossil fuels to hydrogen[4]. The critical issue for hydrogen in general and for aircraft in particular is how to store it. Storage as a solid, liquid or gas, and in-situ production are the four basic options(Watts, 2001). For future aircraft only liquid storage of hydrogen seems to be a realistic option. If air transport can not follow this discontinuity it would rather become a niche market for the traditional organic or fossil fuel suppliers[5].

On the other hand, if hydrogen would become the fuel for future aircraft than we would enter the era of cryogenic storage. Relatively heavy and volume taking pressure vessels would affect the configuration and structural layout of aircraft considerably.

2.3   Scenario/Velocity domains
The aircraft is one of the means to fulfil the transport demands of society. With respect to public transport in economically prosperous areas, different major transport systems will evolve to optimal efficiency, each in a characteristic velocity domain. The optimal transport velocity results from the travelling distance and from the desire and ability of people to invest in travelling time.

Every moving vehicle has to overcome different forms of resistance or drag. The required work, energy, and therefore fuel consumption depends directly on this resistance. The nature of this resistance or drag varies from rolling resistance to aerodynamically induced, friction and wave drag. In order to compare the efficiency of different transport systems in various velocity domains a specific drag (D_{spec}) is introduced. This specific drag is defined as drag per unit total vehicle weight.

Because the specific drag is dependent on speed, some characteristic velocity domains can be defined, see Table 2.

If transport systems for the low, intermediate and high velocity, are selected on a basis of optimal fuel efficiency (as a function of the specific drag value), only three systems are likely to survive for the

[4] China is investing deeply in a hydrogen based economy.

[5] Like general aviation became for supply of aviation gasoline (AVGAS).

local, regional and (inter-) continental markets:

- 'smart' road transport systems;
- high velocity trains; and
- subsonic air transport.

Table 2
Transport systems and fuel efficiency in relation to velocity domains

Proven and future transport systems

Velocity Domain (km/h)[5]	Transport market/system-	Fuel	Dominant resistance/drag-	Specific drag[1] D_{spec}
50 < V < 100	Local: Smart[2] buses Smart[2] cars Smart[2] trains	gas and electricity	wheels (rubber/asphalt) (steel/steel)	$0.01 < D_{spec} < 0.02$
50 < V < 250	Local, regional and continental: human controlled cars buses	liquid fuels	wheels, air friction (rubber/stone)	$0.01 < D_{spec} < 0.20$
125 < V < 300	Regional and continental: high velocity trains	electricity	air friction (steel/steel)	$0.01 < D_{spec} < 0.05$
300 < V < 900 airspeed	Regional, continental and intercontinental subsonic aircraft	liquid fuel, hydrogen	friction drag	$0.08 > D_{spec} > 0.05$[3]

Exotic or obsolete transport systems

V >1000	Intercontinental: supersonic aircraft	liquid fuels	induced drag, wave drag	$0.10 < D_{spec} < 0.15$
V < 150	Regional: wings in ground effect	liquid fuels	air friction, induced drag	$0.20 < D_{spec} < 0.30$
V < 120	Regional: airships	liquid fuels	air friction	$0.025 < D_{spec} < 0.20$[4]

1. D_{spec} = 0·30 (equal to 30%) means: for 1kg in transport about 3N is needed to overcome resistance.
2. Smart could mean:
   - speed and separation controlled,
   - satellite navigation/control, when necessary manual control is overruled,
   - active, instead of heavy passive safety precautions (an enormous reduction of weight).
3. Increasing the cruising altitude reduces the specific drag of aircraft. The result is increased travelling speed.
4. The larger the fineness ratio of an airship, the smaller the specific drag becomes.
5. 1km/h = 0·54 nm/h.

2.4 Scenario/System efficiency of transport vehicles

Improving transport system efficiency is not only challenging for in-novative aerodynamicists and developers of active stability and control systems, but also for structural designers, not as independent development activities but as a joint multi-disciplinary approach. To give an example, the empennage for passive stability and control used in traditional aircraft is a rudiment, a drag and weight increas-

ing leftover. Besides weight reduction through a change in configuration, weight reduction of the system itself is a major challenge.
When the structure efficiency $W_{empty}/W_{payload}$ of different conventional transport vehicles is taken into consideration on a system level,
there is still a big reduction potential.

According to Table 2 aircraft are performing well for continental
transport in terms of their fuel efficiency as a derivative of the specific drag. For intercontinental travelling there is really no alternative, especially when the productivity is taken into account as well.

There is, however, since 1960 a tendency to a continuous rise in airplane cost per seat and a continuous decline in profit per passenger
(Condit, 1996).

The question is how can this process be reversed?

For conventional and optimised aluminium aircraft concepts no
revolutionary improvements are to be expected in the future. The
same appears to be true in the field of traditional aerodynamics and
for measures in stability and control. On the contrary, the cost of
personnel, taxes, insurance and fuel will probably go up. Profits per
passenger seat[6] will decline due to fierce competition in an open sky
market. Therefore, only new aircraft with improved performance
and durability per unit cost could create positive and more competitive perspectives, especially when international environmental regulations are tightened to remove old polluting aircraft. An overall
system weight reduction is possible, e.g. for aircraft from 4 to 3kg
per unit payload, and improved aerodynamic efficiency or the aircraft lift versus drag ratio (L/D), should lead to better performance
per unit weight. In addition, improvement of L/D can be realised by
a change from passive to active (smart) stability and control, in combination with advanced boundary layer control systems, by local porous skin sections in the wing.

New types of energy supply and storage, new aerodynamic aircraft
configurations and a new approach to stability and control will have
to affect the appearance of future aircraft seriously. This will be reflected in future structures, and hence in more durable and sustainable lightweight materials.

2.5 Scenario/Morphologies of structures

The choice of materials in relation to structural concepts is usually
based on the skills of the designers and the company's manufacturing or production traditions. Their material selection is normally very
traditional. When emerging materials and technologies give the opportunity to improve products or even to develop distinguishing

[6] Major airlines claim to have a profit of $5 per passenger on average, equal to $0-05 per kg including luggage. The same profit per kg is claimed for international road transport of frozen meat. Low fare airlines claim profits of $1-2 per pas-senger, which is equal to the profit of one cup of tea sold.

products, local traditions and interests generally frustrate new developments and improvements. In the case of international collaboration programs, local interests and politics are often feeding emotional and technically irrational decisions. Change based on realism is normally hard for the stakeholders, from workers to shareholders, active in the declining old technologies. The aerospace business was and still is a rich source of examples of this phenomenon. In airplane history, nevertheless, several technologies have been overruled by new emerging opportunities.

The first attempts to make flying machines were based on the use of natural materials, like yarns of silk, or flax woven into dense stiff fabrics, taffeta, supported and pre-stressed by 'fingers' of young branches of birch or ash. This gave shape to the lightest possible bird and bat like wing structures, similar to the sketches of Leonardo da Vinci (Fig. 3). Artisans from guilds of weavers, upholsterers and furniture workers thus became the first builders of bird mimicking contraptions.

The same artisan technology was applied to build the glider of Otto Lilienthal, the first successful attempt to mimic soaring birds (Fig. 4). Later on coach and bicycle manufacturers, using primitive industrial processes, made it possible to evolve from the floppy bat-like structures to frames and truss constructions made out of steel wires (tendons), spruce for compression rods (bones) and beams loaded in bending (stems). Firmly pre-tensioned linen was used to upholster spruce ribs, spars and girders to form aerodynamic aerofoils (e.g. the Wright brothers (Fig. 5.)).

High performance plywood laminates made rigid stressed skin wings and fuselages possible (Fokker, Lockheed Vega). These, industrially produced, wooden shell structures were glued with natural starch adhesives. Some time later the change was made to synthetic glues of phenolic resins in order to overcome the temperature and moisture sensibility.

Although the Fokkers, the Lockheed Vegas and the fast and stealthy de Havilland Mosquitos outperformed most contemporary competing metal aircraft, plywood was soon to be replaced by aluminium. Sheets of aluminium were assembled, similar to iron shipbuilding, to form riveted plate structures. Although the introduction of aluminium was purely ideological and political, stressed skins, supported and reinforced by stiffeners and frames, made unforeseen developments possible. The same ideology used to promote aluminium did hamper the introduction of new materials, like composites, in today's civil transport aircraft[7].

[7] This has been different for sailplanes, helicopters, including rotor and propeller blades, military fighters and stealth bombers. Here rationalism is prevailing and composites have largely replaced metals in shell structures. It is likely that geopolitical arguments were overruled by value for money criteria.

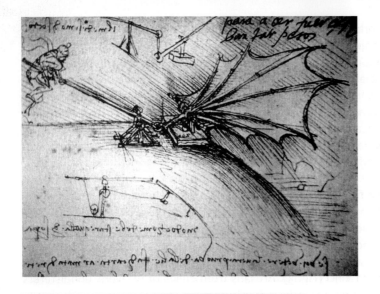

Figure 3
Leonardo da Vinci sketch

Figure 4
Otto Lilienthal

Figure 5
Wright biplane

The arguments used by current metal designers against composites are similar to those used as arguments to support the replacement of wood by metals. These arguments are: a poor understanding of the an-isotropic mechanical behaviour, hard to predict, large scatter in properties, lack of fire resistance, fast degradation, etc. But these arguments are not valid anymore for modern synthetic composites. For example composite plate and shell structures, laminates of fibre-reinforced polymer plies, stacked and cured into solid structures are nowadays predictable and well understood with-respect to mechanical and physical behaviour. In addition modern composites can be fire resistant and verydurable when the ingredients are properly chosen.

2.5.1 Fire safety

Appropriate blending of fibres, polymers and additives improves fire safety considerably[8]. In this way increased burn through retardation of future aircraft structures can be extended to overcome the current evacuation requirements that dominate the cabin layout and number of doors, freeing the way for alternative cabin configurations with fire resistant evacuation corridors as currently applied in modern public buildings.

2.5.2 Weight reduction

Weight reduction can be achieved by the proper exploitation of the improved specific and anisotropic properties, and by the integration of parts and the integration of functions that were previouslyfulfilled by different aircraft elements in the structure.

2.5.3 Production cost reduction

Labour intensive ship building manufacturing techniques applied in the assembly of 'semi-monocoque' stiffened shells in aluminium alloys, can be replaced by labour saving industrially produced textile structures, resulting in purely 'monocoque' structures (like skulls and eggs). Once the textile structures (pre-forms) and foamed core materials are positioned in moulds, including all kinds of local structural elements and even systems (from electromagnetic shielding to sensors, energy and data transport), they can be impregnated using low-pressure techniques. The vacuum bagged structure is finally cured through heating, almost without geometrical and size limitations. The new keywords are parts integration, integration of functions, mechanics and physics, and freedom in geometry without limitations to size. Will the currently accepted curing techniques such as autoclaving in pressurised ovens and pressurised resin transfer moulding become obsolete? Surely not! But they will be used for structures limited in size and mainly used for structures with a demand for specific mechanical performance.

Table 3

The system efficiency of different 'state of the art' metal transport vehicles

State of the art metal transport vehicles	$W_{empty}/W_{payload}$ indicative[3]	
Buses	2·5	
Cars	3 (12)[1]	
	8 (27)[1]	Mercedes Benz S-class, 1st edition, value dominated by propulsion and systems weight
Subsonic aircraft	4[2]	balanced division of weight fractions[3]
Supersonic aircraft	12[2]	value dominated by propulsion, systems and fuel weight
Intercity trains	10[2]	value dominated by structural weight
Global orbit	66	value dominated by fuel weight
Lunar orbit	500	value dominated by fuel weight

1. Between brackets the value is given for one occupant only
2. Values for 70% utilisation
3. $W_{total} = W_{empty} + W_{payload}$
   $W_{empty} = W_{propulsion/systems} + W_{fuel} + W_{structure}$

2.5.4 Improved durability

Durability improvement will be obtained by the elimination of fatigue and corrosion problems. Flight safety will benefit from this as well, although marginal because current failures are mostly caused by human errors, however, equivalent safety levels can be obtained at much lower cost.

2.5.5 Aircraft structures history revisited

The successful replacement of wood by aluminium in the 1930s was based on four presumed improvements:

• fire safety
• weight reduction
• production cost reduction
• improved durability

This belief and the predictability of mechanical properties linked metals to 'science' and 'progress' and made wood 'old-fashioned', even artisan. It was purely rhetorical and not based on research, let alone experience (Condit, 1996). The idea that metal airplanes were 'incombustible' proved to be naïve. Weight appears to be an even more complicated issue as it depends, by nature, on structural efficiency, which in its turn varies with the nature of the loads that structural components have to bear. It took enormous effort to build lighter planes in metal. Buckling, a failure mode based on structural instability in compression, became a new phenomenon and appeared to be a dominant design criterion. Stressed skin concepts could handle shear by diagonal tension. However, diagonals loaded in compression were not weight competitive: thin skin would become unstable and susceptible to buckling. Control of the buckling phenomenon in aircraft resulted in complex locally stiffened aircraft structures with the accompanying high parts count and abundant riveting.

Problems of buckling and durability of aluminium structures like inter-crystalline corrosion and fatigue, were scientifically investigated and either solved or made controllable. When these structural problems were under control, the metal airplane proved to be much more expensive to produce than wooden ones. The reason that the production of metal airplanes was not stopped, originated from the firm belief that mass production of intermediate parts and well organised assembly would reduce the production costs in due time, as in the automotive industry.

[9] Responsible for the low specific drag and high fuel efficiency shown in Table 2.

The wrong initial arguments in favour of the change from wood to aluminium were rapidly overtaken by other, more substantial but rather unexpected advantages such as the pressurisation of the fuselage necessary for high altitude, high-speed, flight[9] combined with aerodynamic smoothness. The capability of the metal airframe in this respect changed large-scale transport by aircraft into a success. Now, after 70 years of improvement and optimisation of aluminium alloys, parts manufacturing and assembly, the traditional metal 'semi-monocoque' structure has reached the stage of consolidation and even decline in the technological life cycle.

The same four arguments that were falsely used to advocate the change from wood to metal aircraft can now be truly used to promote the change from metals to composites for future aircraft structures. To these arguments can be added the crash energy absorbing capability (Formula 1 racing) and the durability and sustainability of composite structures.

2.6 Scenario/Concluding remarks

Concluding the discussion about future scenarios of transport and energy distribution, it is clear that aircraft, especially with improved fuel and transport efficiency, will play a key role in the future for fast and sustainable public transport. New opportunities are arising for aircraft concepts leading to better performance, when advanced fibre reinforced polymer materials and new manufacturing techniques are accepted. The morphology of aircraft structures will change dramatically when the classical role of structures to carry just mechanical loads is revolutionised into a multifunctional and multipurpose role. Therefore, however, it is essential to introduce a new philosophy for structural design, a philosophy where proactive and forward integration and segregation of functions becomes a major design activity.

3. Integration Or Segregation Of Functions As A Future Design Philosophy

Having accepted our scenario for the future, a new design philosophy necessary for new breakthroughs in structural aircraft engineering, is discussed in the next sections. The basis for this new philosophy is the observation that current aircraft are the result of a chain of functional segregation and integration steps that were taken in the evolution of passenger transport aircraft. Being at the end of an evolutionary line we have to travel back along and across the different junctions and choose a different path. A practical approach to this is to make a detailed functional breakdown of the aircraft. New foreseen functions that are not yet installed in today's aircraft should be included, functions no longer valid should be removed.

Having done so, different strategies can be derived, based on different integrations of these functions in the structure. Here we still use the term structure but this should be seen as a 'smart' and 'cooperative' subsystem that learns and monitors and in addition helps other subsystems to do their job. The latter facet is especially important to make improvements possible. Gains in one subsystem should not automatically be used to make that subsystem optimal but can be 'given' to other subsystems where maybe a higher leverage on the improvement can be obtained.

The structure should no longer be seen as a passive static subsystem, which just functions as a backbone for other subsystems. A structure can be made smart to take over functions of other subsystems. Likewise, functions of the structure can be transferred to other subsystems if they have a better way of meeting a system demand.

This can be illustrated when we look at fuselages of aircraft. During the evolution of passenger transport aircraft, different segregation steps have been made. The first important decision was to divide payload containment and lift generation from each other. Today's aircraft are drag-raising tubes kept in the air with a set of wings.

The next important segregation was the division between payload containment and stability. Large tail sections are needed to keep the aircraft in a stable flight. These tail sections use our flying tube as a load path, imposing a complex set of extra loads and systems. The next important step was the segregation of the propulsion system from all other aircraft systems. The current under wing mounted, pylon-supported engines pods are considered optimal for certain aspects. However, one could also see this solution as an oversegregated interpretation of Cayley's philosophy to separate propulsion from lift generation.

The engines can be regarded just as mechanical, acoustic and thermal load generators. Not having to cope with their presence in the tube is handy for the structural designers but it can be seriously questioned if it does not serve the overall system performance best. Especially as one considers the future demands on noise and pollution.

If we bring these demands back into the list of potential functions of the fuselage we can start thinking of a whole range of new solutions. We shall come back to this later.

Let's first look at what technology offers and promises for the next decades.

The structural designers play with materials, production technology and shape. Materials in this context should be regarded as both passive and active materials. We can distinguish load carrying, supporting and protecting materials. The structures are arrangements of materials, having production methods as a constraint or as an enabler, such that functions can be fulfilled. In its simplest form, concepts are related to strength or stiffness optimisation. In its most advanced form concepts could be constellations of materials that fulfil a large set of mechanical and non-mechanical functions and that are able to monitor or even heal themselves.

The bases for all concepts are materials and production technology. Naturally, the developments of materials and production technology can be initiated based on imaginary concepts, where materials are described by imaginary potential and can be made into structures with imaginary processes.

The integration scenario chosen is largely influenced by constraints such as available volume, weight budgets and costs. There will be a major difference between small and large aircraft in that sense. If we compare two of the latest aircraft, the Extra 400 and the Airbus A380, it becomes clear that integration strategies are completely different.

3.1   Small aircraft

In small aircraft, like the Extra 400 (Fig. 6), internal volume and noise levels dominate the level of comfort. Integrating choices should be based on maximisation of the internal volume and minimisation of the noise level. The structural designer can support this objective by designing for minimisation of fuselage wall thickness (wall is used to indicate complete thickness of skin, stiffeners and frames) and improving sound insulation as much as possible. The result is a sandwich structure with a very limited number of stiffeners and frames that can cope with a pressurised non-circular cross-section.

3.2 Large aircraft

For large aircraft, like the A380 (Fig. 7), the situation is completely different. Although here passenger comfort is also dominated by space and noise, the structural designer cannot take the path followed for small aircraft. Space in large aircraft is much more dominated by seat pitch than headroom. Since seat pitch is simply dominated by passenger willingness to spend money, the designer can't help much here. What can be done is to aim for noise reduction and structural improvements to help achieve the overall goal of weight reduction.

This application of integration and segregation can be applied to a much wider range of aircraft functions.

Below, a possible scenario is discussed that will be used as a guideline for future material and structural developments.

3.3 Future large aircraft

A conceptual scenario for a future aircraft configuration with a great potential is taken off the shelf:

3.3.1 Blending of the fuselage with the wing into an aircraft without a tail

Famous aircraft designers like the Horten brothers, Lee, Jones and Jack Northrop were strong supporters of the flying wing concept. They realised that the tail section or empennage of traditional aircraft is responsible for quite a lot of 'parasitic' drag and 'dead' weight. Distribution of pay-load in the lift generation sections, as is usual for fuel, will lead to lower bending and torsion moments, especially in the centre section, and as a consequence to a lighter construction. In addition, due to the enormous cross-sectional area of the inner wing box, the bending and torsion stresses will decrease as well. Since the beginning of the 1950s flying wings lost attention until John Northrop's visionary ideas became airborne as the tailless B-2 bomber (1988) (Fig. 8).

Controlled stable flight was realised artificially by fly-by-wire and active computer control. Research programs to make the concept applicable for civil aircraft were initiated after the successful introduction of the B-2. Special attention was given to the problem of how to integrate a pressurised passenger cabin and how to store fuel, freight and passengers safe and happy[10].

According to recent European and American studies (Liebeck, Page and Rawdon, 1998) a change from a conventional 800 passenger configuration to a tailless blended wing body (BWB) configuration will result in the following prime benefits:

[10] Installation of an artificial window in front of each passenger, can solve the lack of or even the disappearance of windows in aircraft, it offers a personal window to the world and all media.

- fuel burn 27% lower,
- take off weight 15% lower,
- empty weight 12% lower,
- total thrust 27% lower,
- lift to drag ratio, L/D 20% higher.

Figure 6
Extra 400

Figure 7
Airbus A380

Figure 8
Northrop Grumman B-2 Spirit

The group of NASA researchers (Liebeck, Page and Rawdon, 1998) concluded with the following memorable words:

"The magnitude of performance increments of the blended wing body (BWB) over the conventional baseline airplane is indeed unusual, if not unprecedented, in the aircraft industry. All of these benefits are due to the BWB configuration itself, rather then specific traditional technologies such as aerodynamics or structures." (See Fig. 9).

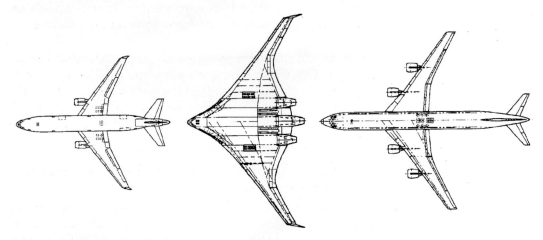

3.3.2   BWB potential in numbers

The initial basis for the NASA comparison study was the following set of performance requirements (Liebeck, Page and Rawdon, 1998):

Figure 9
Planview of conventional and BWB configurations.

- capacity: 800 passengers in three-class seating,
- range: 7,000nm or 13,000 km,
- cruise speed: Mach 0·85,
- take off field length: 11,000ft or 3,630m, and
- the application of advanced ducted fan technology.

For a conventional 800 seat aircraft about 4,250m² of 'wet' aerodynamic surface is required to encapsulate sufficient volume for lift. When an 85m wingspan is applied, an aerodynamic aircraft efficiency L/D 21 is possible. In the case of a blended wing body configuration several studies have shown that for an equal number of passengers, requiring 2m³ living space per passenger, the total

required 'wet' surface is reduced by 30% to 3,000m2 (dematerialisation by a configuration change). With the same wingspan, a 20% improvement of the aircraft aerodynamic efficiency L/D to 25 is the result of putting the payload in a body that is generating lift as well.

Maintaining a profile thickness of 15% results in a wing centre section four floors high. Even if the structural efficiency is still the same compared to traditional aircraft, for a 13,000km or 7,000nm flying distance, a fuel consumption reduction of 38% can be realised and that counts. Instead of four, three engines are sufficient which leads to an additional 15% of weight reduction.

In addition a unique structural performance per unit weight and cost can be realised by the introduction of new structural solutions. So for an equal number of passengers and similar required volume, even more aircraft performance improvements can be realised.

To design and build three-dimensionally curved aerodynamic structures containing lightweight pressurised cells for passengers, (with good ergonomic, fire and crash safety performance), is an opportunity for lightweight fibre reinforced polymer structures, blended and supported by structures made of aluminium, titanium and steel.

3.4 Future 'frozen' textile structures, from filament and yarn to lightweight structures

The greatest benefit for future textile structures is the sustainable way of manufacturing large structures. Starting with simple intermediates, like bobbins of yarns, tapes, fabrics and resins, a series of textile pre-forms can be manufactured and assembled into a tailor made 'cloth' representing the 'core of the structure'. Impregnation with a resin takes place before, during or after the fibre placement stage in a mould. A final cure at low pressure (vacuum) in an oven (no size limitations) is all that remains. This procedure, where different fibre/textile placement machines can play a role, is the ultimate form of 'down stream manufacturing'. It means a maximum reduction of intermediate steps between basic material selection (the ingredients) and product realisation (the cooking). If the steel and aluminium mills could produce steel and aluminium yarns and as a derivative metal textiles, an infinite number of new advanced applications for metals would arise. The unprecedented formability of textiles makes complex large three-dimensional curved shell structures possible, unlimited in size and given shape with textile fibre placement techniques, like weaving, braiding, tape laying and filament winding (see Fig. 10). By extending the existing families of fibre materials, like glass and carbon, with yarns of metal fibres, any mechanical, physical and electro-magnetic property can be created by blending. In textile terms, this can be done by inter-mingling and co-mingling of fibres and yarns. If we classify a few fibres (existing and futuristic) for application in curved shell structures, the following listing for different structural elements can be made with respect to the mechanical performance per unit weight (the structure efficiency). The starting point for comparison is an equal volume of fibres and equal fibre architectures. The results are related to imaginary yarns of high performance aluminium or steel filaments, equal in thickness and with a similar imaginary fibre to matrix adhesion).

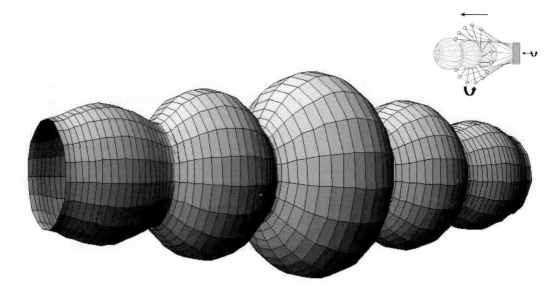

Figure 10
Multiple winding shapes

Table 4 shows that for large shell structures, manufactured in a cost effective way using technologies that can handle continuous fibre reinforced composites, the best mechanical performance per unit weight is realised by the use of carbon fibres. In the case of a filament wound or braided segmented iso-tensoid pressure vessel, applicable for pressurised cabins or cryogenic fuel containers, a carbon fibre reinforced version performs 12·9 times better than the aluminium wound version. Compared to a steel fibre reinforced vessel a factor of 5·2 makes the difference. When the numbers are inverted, then the relative weight per unit performance is compared to the least attractive material choice.

For flat and simply curved plate structures the numbers are totally different, because the engineering properties for metal plates (the ideal morphology for this kind of structures) remain similar in all directions (the fibres are fused into an isotropic metal matrix). For a simple composite plate, like a (0-90) degrees laminate of fibre reinforced epoxy (strong fibres in a weak matrix) and a fibre volume fraction of 0·5, the engineering constants reduce to a level of about 25%. Also the density of the composite material will change following the rule of mixtures. Anyhow, when the same calculations are made for plate structures, once again carbon fibre reinforced materials give the best results, but less pronounced. So after the selection of the most attractive fibres for composite plate and shell structures from a mechanical standpoint, we have to consider the other system requirements as well.

Table 4

Structure efficiency or performance per unit weight, for different existing and imaginary yarn materials, materialised into a few typically loaded structural members. The values are relative to the lowest registered value[11]

Structure efficiency or Performance per unit weight	based on imaginary yarn properties of equal apperance	engineering constants	carbon fibre yarns existing T 300	glass fibre yarns existing E-type	alufibre yarn virtual 7075	steel fibre yarn virtual piano wire
Material properties	density	ρ 10^3 kgm^{-3}	1·76	2·58	2·70	7·80
	Young's modulus	E 10^9 Nm^{-2}	230	73	71	210
	yield stress	σ_y 10^6 Nm^{-2}	3,530	3450	420	3100
Structure efficiency relative (vs) the lowest listed value (1·0)		**dominant parameter**				
Solid shells: compression	buckling critical	$(E^{1/3}/\rho)$ vs $(E^{1/3}/\rho)_{min}$	4·5	2·1	2·0	1·0
Curved beams: Compression Bending	buckling critical or stiffness critical strength critical	$(E^{1/2}/\rho)$ vs $(E^{1/2}/\rho)_{min}$	4·7	1·8	1·7	1·0
Bending		$(\sigma_f^{2/3}/\rho)$ vs $(\sigma_f^{2/3}/\rho)_{min}$	4·1	4·1	1·0	3·9
Pressure vessels:	strength critical, iso-tensoid wound	(σ/ρ) vs $(\sigma/\rho)_{min}$	12·9	8·6	1·0	2·5
Sandwich shells: Bending	stiffness critical	(E/ρ) vs $(E/\rho)_{min}$	4·8	1·0	1·0	1·0

[11] The yield stress is the lowest stress at which a material undergoes plastic deformation or failure, the magnitudes mentioned are rather academic and unaffected by any degradation.

4. Multidisciplinary Aircraft Design

For structures dominated by stiffness or strength, the potential of aluminium alloys to improve the mechanical performance of aircraft structures has been explored almost completely. A change to new morphologies, from solid plates and profiles to fibre metal laminates or even wires and fabrics, offers the possibility for new hybrid potentials with improved specific static and dynamic mechanical (fatigue) properties.

Just replacing a material in order to save weight, for example aluminium on a one to one basis by carbon fibre reinforced epoxy (black metal structures), is the most easy but foolish approach thinkable. It ignores extreme possible dangers due to the different characters of material response to local overloading or to design failures (a relative friendly and slow cracking of metals versus a nasty and explosive de-bonding or disintegration of composites). It ignores also the fact that if we want to replace a proven and cheap metal solution by a composite version we can only compete on a value for money basis.

4.1   Technology growth curves

To consolidate proven technologies on the threshold of their decline, companies make huge investments for only marginal improvements in order to stay ahead of the emerging and more potential technologies. However, it is a known phenomenon that in the stage of decline in the technology life cycle, 'optimisation' leads only to minor improvements (see Fig. 11). Every improvement e.g. in metal yield or failure stress, has trade offs with respect to fatigue or corrosion resistance. All modifications and new formulations within one material family leave the modulus of elasticity, which is so important for light and stiffness dominated structures (deflection or buckling critical), mostly unaffected. So in general, large improvements are only achieved by the introduction of more potent material families, in pursuit of better specific properties and more attractive manufacturing possibilities to make structures with higher added value. These last arguments are also important because newly developed materials and their technology are almost by definition more expensive than the traditional ones they compete with and threaten to replace. Thus adding as much value for money as possible is the leading principle.

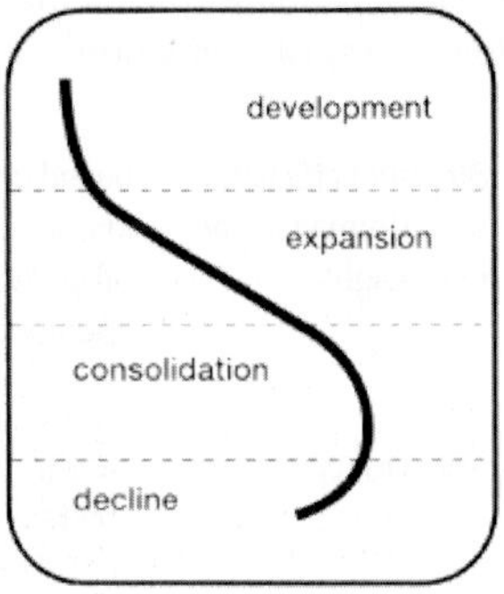

Figure 11
The S curve

4.2   Improved performance and cheaper to manufacture

If we have to select the most challenging and, for renewal, the most attractive part for multidisciplinary design, then the pressurised fuselage in a conventional aircraft or the passenger compartment in a flying wing is the ultimate candidate. This subassembly is the heaviest, the most expensive and, by the number of parts and assembly, the most complex structure of all.

5.   Multi-disciplinary Design For Fuselages, Integration Of Mechanics And Acoustics

The starting point for the choice of new combinations of materials, structural concepts and manufacturing technologies should be the improvement of the efficiency by integration of functions. The next diagram shows schematically which requirements have to be fulfilled for the development and design of aircraft fuselage structures. Along the horizontal axis the most important structural design and material requirement categories are shown. The level of function integration during manufacturing realised by the structural design concept, is plotted along the vertical axis. The envelopes 'waving away' from the origin represent families of materials, structures and technologies with a growing potential for function integration. When properly done the result is a more competitive structure. In practice, however, structural design is characterised by a number of sequential activities with poor interaction. Optimisation is usually achieved only with respect to stiffness and strength of the structure. At the end the fulfilment of physical requirements, like thermal and acoustical insulation, is achieved by adding cladding of insulating and vibration reducing elements, at the cost of labour, weight and money for materials.

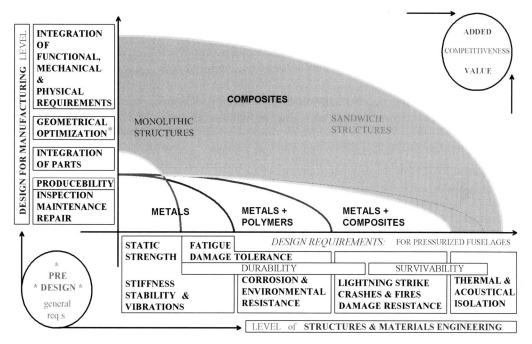

Figure 12
Fuselage requirements

The philosophy of renewed segregation and integration will now be applied in the design of composite fuselages to explore a few basic potential improvements. First the influence of a very elementary design parameter, the frame pitch, on the metal and composite fuselage weight is investigated.

The structural efficiency of a fuselage section reinforced by frames and stiffeners reinforced can be judged by the section weight as a function of the frame pitch and skin thickness in relation to sufficient strength and stability, an elementary and lean set of 'design graphs' is presented on the next page All the design curves have the same characteristic form. Below a certain frame pitch the fuselage weight is constant and governed by the maximum allowable material stress.

Above this frame pitch the fuselage weight is governed by the stability of the skin panels. In the stability critical region an increase in frame pitch is only possible with growing skin thickness, as a result the stress level in the fuselage decreases. The lightest possible fuselages are the fuselages with the thinnest skins when we forget about physical requirements. It can be seen that the lightest aluminium fuselage is about 30% heavier than the lightest carbonepoxy fuselage (Fig. 13a).

The figure shows also that a new and larger design window appears when we change from metal to carbon-epoxy composites. This window for frame pitch selection allows us to create structures equal or lower in weight than metal ones in which we can apply a renewed segregation and integration to fulfil the fuselage requirements.

Here we will explore the potential of the integration and segregation of acoustic and thermal insulation in the mechanical design of fuselages.

6.   Sound Insulation In Aircraft Fuselages

The sound insulation of a fuselage depends on many parameters, for instance the noise source spectrum incident on the fuselage, the resonance frequencies of the fuselage structure and the pressure difference between the inside and outside of the fuselage. To get an impression of the effect of the structural parameters on the sound insulation, it is sufficient to consider a flat stiffened panel with identical air conditions on both sides.

The reduction in noise transmission is characterised by the so-called transmission loss (TL). Sacrificing some of the weight savings achieved by exchanging aluminium with composites can improve the acoustical insulation of a stiffened shell fuselage. In the set of figures below is shown that the carbon epoxy fuselage has the potential to improve the sound insulation with 1·4dB, equal to a 30% noise reduction, by a 'simple' increase of the frame pitch from the conventional 20in or 500mm to 1,330mm So the acoustical insulation can be improved by increasing the frame pitch and by increasing the skin thickness. These adjustments lead both to a reduction of parts and lower stress levels having as consequence better resistance against impact and damage tolerance. If we neglect the new measures necessary to support systems and interior parts it becomes clear that the weight, the production and maintenance cost of an aircraft with such a fuselage decreases, e.g. due to a 50% reduction of frames. An intelligent exploitation of the composite fuselage design window can make this aircraft more competitive with the conventional aluminium aircraft, than the aircraft equipped with the lightest possible composite fuselage (see Fig. 13).

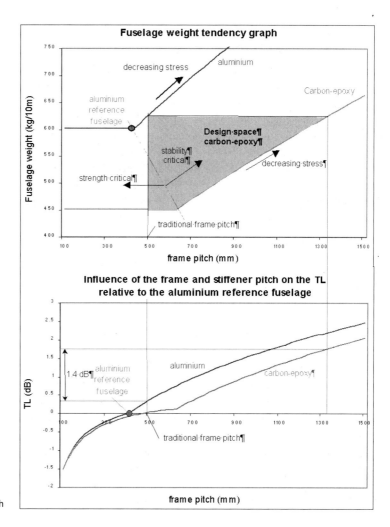

Figure 13
The effects of fuselage frame pitch

Until now only the stiffened skin structural concept was discussed. A different structural concept is the sandwich concept. For sandwich panels, two skins separated by core with a very low density, no stiffeners are needed. Therefore no mass will be lost in stiffeners, resulting in a relatively high value of mass per unit area of the skin, which results in a better TL according to the mass law. Also, the core can be made of a material with high insulating acoustic and thermal properties. The number of discrete stiffeners can then be minimised, since they are only required at places where high concentrated forces are introduced (wing, landing gear, etc.) or diverted (e.g. from cut-outs). This can reduce the production and maintenance cost. The potential of the sandwich concept for integrated design will now be elaborated.

7. Integration Of Mechanics And Acoustics In The Sandwich Fuselage Concept

Two sandwich design strategies can be distinguished for optimal integration of mechanics and acoustical insulation (Kurtze and Watters, 1954).

The first strategy is to choose a high coincidence frequency and follow the mass law as long as possible. This can be achieved using a core material with a very low shear modulus. The second strategy is to choose a core material with a high shear modulus so the core will behave like an incompressible material. The high shear modulus of the core makes this sandwich more structurally efficient.

The major disadvantage of this strategy is that the coincidence frequency will be relatively low. Of these two strategies the one which will give the best result depends on the noise source and on the structural requirements for the sandwich shells.

The potential of the sandwich structure for improved acoustic insulation is shown in the figure above where it can be seen that the stiffness of the sandwich can be varied between maximum stiffness (infinitely shear stiff core) and minimum stiffness (zero stiffness core). The acoustical insulation can be improved by shifting the coincidence frequency above the frequency range important for speech. Depending on the core material used in the sandwich skin, the fuselage will be structurally efficient (core material with a high shear modulus), or acoustically efficient (core material with a low shear modulus). The design choice is dependent on the noise source and the stress levels in the sandwich fuselage structure.

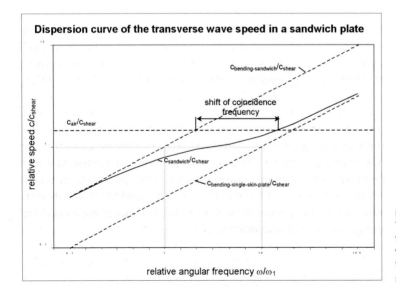

Dispersion curve of the transverse wave speed in a sandwich plate

$C_{bending-sandwich}/C_{shear}$

shift of coincidence frequency

C_{air}/C_{shear}

$C_{sandwich}/C_{shear}$

$C_{bending-single-skin-plate}/C_{shear}$

relative speed c/C_{shear}

relative angular frequency ω/ω_1

Figure 14
The shift of the coincidence frequency for a sandwich panel with a bending stiffness of 20 times the stiffness of a single skin plate and $\omega_2/\omega_1 = 10^{(7)}$

Another interesting aspect of the sandwich concept is the possibility to integrate thermal insulation into the fuselage structure. Materials with a low conductivity, which can also meet the structural demands, are polymer foams, which are also very efficient as sandwich core materials.

Concluding, one could say that the application of the sandwich concept offers great possibilities of fulfilling requirements in an integrated way.

8. Sound & Climate Management In Future Aircraft Structures

After these simple examples of the segregation–integration philosophy discussed in the previous sections, we can now try to apply the idea to future aircraft configurations. In this section an attempt is made to do this for the blended wing body concept, taking into consideration the main areas that demand improvement.

Reduction of aircraft noise is a major current and future issue. Improved internal and external sound management, the war against noise, becomes more and more important for airliners and airports.

8.1 Exterior noise

Severe noise restrictions in populated areas, especially during take off, will impose developments to improve the aircraft aerodynamic efficiency and the aircraft structural efficiency.

The flying wing or blended wing body concept has the potential to improve the aerodynamic efficiency by 20%. If made from carbon composite an improvement in structural efficiency of 25% can be realised.

Combining this with improved flight management, e.g. steeper take off and landing with reduced propulsion, the projected noise intensity footprints on the ground can be minimised.

8.2 Interior noise

Intercontinental travellers would appreciate reduced sound intensity levels in the cabin as well. The flying wing concept offers room to encapsulate the main source of exterior airborne noise, the ultra high bypass jet engines, in the wing sections (Fig. 15). The engine duct gives the possibility to reduce the noise of the propulsion by using sound absorbing liner materials and a maximised flow of cold bypass air. It will make insulation of the cabin area from this external source easier. The sound transmitted by the structure itself is controlled and reduced by damping flexible mounts and supports. For the BWB fuselage a large degree of function separation can be applied. This will lead to newly defined structural elements: an exterior aerodynamic structure and an internal cellular segmented structure. The external skin will be used for system support, aerodynamic load carrying and crash load absorption; the internal cells will be used for the pressurised and isolated (thermal and acoustic) fire proof transport of passengers; similar cells will be used as fuel containers and freight compartments.

The new structural elements are made from different materials. The external skin is built up from carbon fibre reinforced polymers blended with metallic fibres and special fillers to fulfil all the durability and survivability requirements (lightning strike, crashes, fires and impact). The internal structure is made from iso-tensoid filament wound vessels with variable diameters which can be interconnected and interfering where necessary. Materials are selected to get an airtight, fire proof and proper isolated structure.

By mounting energy supply, data supply and control systems in the non-pressurised sections of the cabin and wing structure very special sound reduction measures in the soft mounted 'monocoque' passenger compartment can be obtained. The bending stiff sandwich structures will assure sound isolation for high frequencies. For the low frequencies the degree of insulation is proportional to added mass but this approach is against the desire and nature of aircraft structural design. The multi leaf partition structure, a result of function segregation, is used. This is not only a measure in the war against noise but it also leaves room for the application of sound absorbing soft and porous visco-elastic polymer layers, as part of the sandwich cabin structure. Both measures will cause additional transmission loss, the latter by absorbing low frequency sound waves and converting them into heat.

Possible results are shown in Fig. 15 above and below. Here a cross-section of a future blended wing body aircraft is presented where the main trends and potential answers observed in this article are interpreted. Although not all shown in detail, the main items in this cross-section are: integration of engines and hydrogen storage in the blended volume, segregation of pressurised volume from the volume required to obtain aerodynamic shape, separation of cold and air conditioned aircraft areas, insulation of sound for the passenger by segregation of payload areas from mechanically vibrating sections, and integration or segregation of service aisles and fire escape routes.

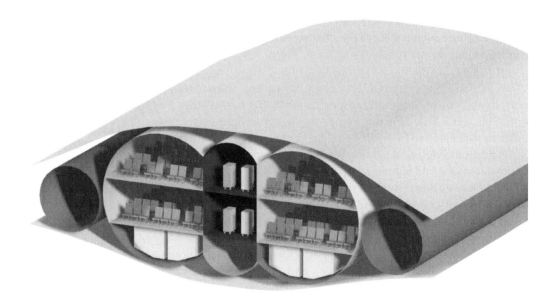

Figure 15
BWB fuselage cross-section

9. Passenger Cabin Lay-outs

The segmented cellular cells in series are filament wound or braided. Chains like this can be nested in many ways, varying from a small interference to a tight interference. In the first solution gates are connect one cell to another (Fig. 16a). In case of the tight interference foam alike, a single multi dome space can be created (Fig. 16c). Like a cathedral with partition walls, the floors and pillars are all loaded in tension caused by the geometry and internal pressurisation.

As opposed to cathedrals and mosques with domed ceilings, where compression dominates caused by gravity, our proposed passenger cabin structures are mainly loaded in pure tension, due to the fibre reinforcing architecture or load path strategy, the internal pressurisation and last but not least the incredible structural lightness.

10. Conclusions

In the first chapters we asked whether future air transport is relevant and sustainable and which energy supply technologies could play a viable role in the long term. In the future, subsonic aircraft performance will be improved tremendously and become more sustainable, especially when international environmental regulations are tightened. For public transport over long distances there is no other transport system that can compete with aircraft, unless people are willing to invest, en masse, in travelling time, in days instead of hours. Even in the high subsonic velocity domains the fuel efficiency per unit weight in combination with the high productivity of aircraft makes them competitive with all other types of transport.

Although the structural efficiency of contemporary aircraft is not bad a lot of improvement is still possible especially when flying wing configurations do emerge.

When in the future hydrogen technology will emerge in road transport, it might be used for air transport as well[12]. If it is, then the layout of aircraft will be affected tremendously. When lightweight solutions are developed for hydrogen-tight containers with good thermo-insulating properties, iso-tensoid fibre reinforcement strategies will result in safe and lightweight pressure vessel configurations for a failsafe energy dense hydrogen storage. The same principle of using segmented and variable diameter filament-wound or braided structures is applicable for the pressurised passenger cabin. Different nesting strategies of the vessels are possible and when a strong interference solution is chosen the interior becomes a multi dome hall with a skin, partition walls, pillars and floors loaded in pure tension (aircraft engineering becomes architectural engineering). Because the fibre controlled structure is mainly loaded in tension, the cost of maintenance will be low.

[12] On the other hand the use of liquid fossil or bio fuels could be far more practical if a worldwide low-cost fuel supply is guaranteed and future environmental rules are met.

Weight reduction of the load carrying shell as a single activity is useless and dangerous. The shell must become a system to transport payload safely and comfortably, hence all the interacting functions must be considered together, i.e. strength, fatigue life, noise and thermal insulation, safety and survivability.

Textile reinforced polymers, from the fibre level to the shell structure, tuneable for any requested property, are the only candidate materials. A proper integration or segregation of functions and requirements will lead to the ultimate performance and durability per unit weight. The sandwich structure concept will dominate over the stiffened shell, especially when thermal and acoustic insulation are important factors.

Together with the aerodynamic improvement, encapsulated high bypass jet engines will result into low noise generating transport. The rear part of the engine duct might become a processor of exhaust gases as well as nucleating water vapour into falling rainwater.

The problems that will surely arise in the materialisation and operation of new aircraft concepts, are challenges for a new generation of scientists and engineers. Good (scientific) education, an open mind and a enterprising attitude will be crucial, to follow the example of what the Wright brothers did 100 years ago.

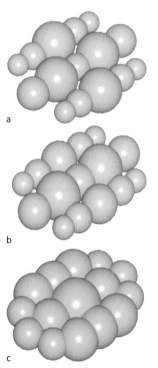

a

b

c

Figure 16
Nests of pressure vessels from pressurised tubes to nested chains of ellipsoidal segments and pressurised 'cathedrals'

References

Watts, P. Exploring the Future — Energy Needs, Choices and Possibilities — Scenarios to 2050, 2001, Shell International, London.

Torenbeek, E. We Nemen een Schoon vel Tekenpapier (in Dutch), 2000, Delft University Press, ISBN 90-407-2112-2.

Condit P.M. Airline costs on the rise while yield slips, 1996, AIAA World Aviation Conference, Los Angeles, 1996.

Wooden airplanes in the United States, 1920-1945, Technology and Culture, 1994, 35, (1), pp 34-69.

Liebeck, R.H., Page, M.A. and Rawdon, B.K. Blended-wing-body subsonic commercial transport, AAIA-98-0438, 1998.

Krakers, L.A., Van Tooren, M.J.L., Beukers, A. and Bergsma, O.K. Multi-disciplinary fuselage design: Integration of mechanics and acoustics, 2000, SAMPE Europe Conference, Paris, 2000., pp 617-622.

Kurtze, G. and Watters, B.G. New wall design for high transmission loss or high damping, 1954, J Acoustical Soc of America, 31, (6).

M.A. Luke Lowings introduced his paper as an approach "that tries to argue for other than 'quantifiable' criteria in judging and developing designs". He is principal of Carpenter/Lowings Architecture & Design and in this series of papers he was invited to claim the role of the artistic architect. Every building, its structure, space and material are located in a specific architectural and urban setting. Besides functional necessities, the building envelope within its particular location calls for a careful approach to strengthen the connection between the building and the human environment.

The Future Envelope 1 – A Multidisciplinary Approach. U. Knaack and T. Klein (Eds.). IOS Press, 2008.

OVERLAPPING BOUNDARIES

Luke Lowings

Carpenter/Lowings A & D, London

1.   Introduction

James Carpenter and I have spent many years with our colleagues (most notably Richard Kress), first in New York and now also in London exploring the possibilities of integrating visual ideas involving light into built space. Our interest in the relationship between people and their environment (which is most frequently manifested in the form of daylight) has developed into a general concern with the boundary condition - whether between inside and outside, or between parts of a large building, or at the perimeter of an area of land – and this has grown naturally into a concern with the envelope of buildings. We have been asked on a number of occasions over this period to help develop part (or all) of the envelope of a building and our role at the boundary of the discipline of architecture itself has enabled us to seek creative solutions to some of the issues, while our collaborative approach has proved helpful in working on the complex nexus of issues involved. All the technical aspects of an efficient envelope – structurally and in terms of environmental control – must be synthesized with this idea of connecting the user to his or her environment.

The future is unpredictable. We think that the envelope will evolve in a number of different ways: there will be almost as many solutions to the question of what to do with the exterior of a building as there are projects. Every envelope can provide a unique opportunity. This constant proliferation of designs could be said to correspond to Darwin's concept of random mutation, some of which prove more successful than others in different contexts – the 'survival of the fittest', so to speak. These successful variants will become the precursors of 'species' of façade that will be refined and developed and produce further 'mutations' in the future. The process of change never rests, and only in retrospect is it possible to say that one particular species represents the qualities of the 'zeitgeist'. It is not only the fittest from a 'technical' point of view that will survive, since architecture exists in a complex cultural context: there are also aesthetic considerations and it is often the design that synthesizes disparate considerations that proves most durable, rather than the extreme case, which simply serves to illustrate an evolutionary dead end.

However, it is interesting to look at the various 'mutations' of the façade and try to categorize them, with the intention of identifying the genesis of potential new 'species'. What follows is not intended as a survey of all the possible envelope types, but within some work that we have been involved in there may be the seeds of some future directions.

The projects that I will describe are all different solutions to different problems and I will not attempt to try to make them all into a single body of work; they are more a series of reflections on the conditions prevalent in their environment; physical, cultural, economic - but I hope that together they reflect a common set of concerns that will become evident.

As we know the paradigm of transparency has lost its potency. It was one of the drivers of the development of early modern architecture as a metaphor for freedom, intellectual clarity, and an easy relationship to the natural world which was usually deemed to be 'outside' the construct of the built world. The simplistic distinction between 'man-made' environments and 'natural' environments has been long discredited – we, and all our cultural constructs, are part of the 'natural' world, just one of many interdependent systems. The envelope is a permeable membrane, when seen in relation to light, sound, heat, moisture. As has been observed many times before, the ideal of visual transparency is, in any event, rarely achieved: even with large unbroken areas of clear single-glazed glass and a distinctly 'natural' environment outside, glass is only transparent under certain light conditions.

A great deal of hope has been put in the development of coatings, laminates, and various specialized types of glass to solve the inherent problems of poor thermal performance and fragility that glass as a material brings with it, and these developments continue, but it is clear that the concept of the all-glass building has not kept up with demands that it should conserve energy. Recent regulations in Europe have made the all-glass façade extremely difficult to achieve so architects who might have previously striven for the simplicity of a glass façade have to face the problem of what to do instead. We were never interested exclusively in the concept of transparency, but have tried to use refraction, reflectivity, translucency and layering to enlarge the depth of the boundary, so we feel that our work to date is of particular relevance to the current situation.

From top to bottom

Figure 1-6
The Rachofsky House
Dichroic Light Field
Tower Palace London

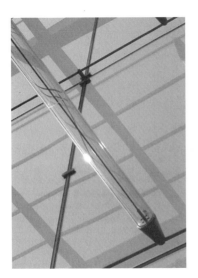

2.   Cable-net facades:

At the extreme end of the spectrum of 'transparency' in our recent work, lie the Jazz at Lincoln Center/Columbus Centre cable net walls. These provide a 46m high all-glass façade, in an extremely difficult location at a very busy traffic junction at the south-west corner of Central Park in New York. It has a wonderful location at the western end of Central Park South and from inside there are indeed views to 'nature' above treetop height over the Park as well as down the axis of the street. The solution was complicated by the need to provide acoustic isolation for the interior where jazz performances are not only played but also recorded. The initial desire was to have an expression of the space (the foyer to the more traditional concert hall within the body of the building), on the exterior façade. We realized that this would involve at least triple-glazing the façade with the accompanying heavyweight structure destroying the transparent effect, so we proposed a two-layer solution. On the exterior a single-laminated glass façade on a two-way cable net is suspended from a twenty-five metre truss that bridges the axial space between the twin towers behind. Inside, a second independent, inclined, single-laminated façade with vertical cables only, is hung from the same truss immediately behind the outer one. The variety of thicknesses of the glass, and the interlayers, and the physical separation of the two walls preserves the acoustic isolation of the performance space from the street outside. The separation from the retail space immediately below is not as thorough of course, since there is only one façade between it and the performance space but the noise levels during performance times are such that this is not a problem.

The cable-net at Columbus Centre was developed from our design for the façade of the German Foreign Ministry which in turn was developed from the work of Schlaich Bergermann and Partner at the Kempinsky Hotel in Munich and their work with cable structures of many years. We tried in the Foreign Ministry to make more explicit the boundary condition of the façade: separating the two layers of cables; introducing dichroic elements and a semi-reflective coating in the central area of the façade to work with the daylight, that renders the façade quite reflective at most times of day. From the exterior the central reflective area to the façade appears as a floating surface surrounded by a clear border. These minimal interventions on the façade were combined with reflective surfaces to the overhead beams to create a subtle shimmering of light and reflection that dissolves the boundary under some light conditions. It was interesting to us that the expressed intention of the façade in this location was to make the building more 'accessible' to the public and visually per-

Figure 7-12
Columbus Center, Glass Wall and Roof
New York, USA| Building architect: Skidmore, Owings & Merrill |
Design engineer: Schlaich, Bergermann & Partner
1999-2004

Figure 13-16
Lichthof Facade and Roof
German Foreign Ministry, Berlin |
Building architect: Müller Reimann
Architekten | Engineer: Schlaich,
Bergermann & Partner
1999

meable, but that also the glass had to withstand the impact of a car at ground level and to be totally secure at all times, in other words: one should be able to look in but the boundary must be totally controlled, an unconscious description of the boundaries of the modern western state. In architectural terms, this project came to describe the paradox at the heart of the 'transparent' façade.

3.   Thin Facades:

The problem of the façade in a typical western office building is one that has been a subject of debate in recent years. Mies Van der Rohe's paradigmatic curtain wall in the Seagram building produced a thousand imitations and the ideal of floor to ceiling transparency from the inside is still a default position for letting agents in London and New York at least, although new energy saving regulations make this more and more difficult to achieve despite coatings advances. More stringent requirements in the 1990's in parts of Europe (and a longer-term commercial view than in the US?) resulted in a lot of work on double-skinned facades which seemed to reclaim the envelope for architects and engineers as a field for creative endeavor, but the commercial pressures on rentable area and the questionable effectiveness of some of these solutions, mean that alternatives have been sought, particularly when the space for two skins is not available and the initial capital investment and maintenance costs must be kept low.

We have recently worked on two projects that addressed this problem in two different ways for different reasons. The first in New York is an example of a relatively simple clear glass façade that is refined to be as elegant and efficient as possible. It is for the main curtain wall of the World Trade Seven building at the northern edge of the site that was mostly destroyed in the events of September 11th 2001. Initial ideas of double-skin facades, integrated chilled slabs and other systems that are not viewed as outlandish in Europe but which are extremely rare in the US were shelved in order to maximize floor areas and minimize capital outlay, so the façade is as thin as it can be, and the visual idea is developed from an attempt to minimize the visual effect of the deep ceiling/floor voids that the air-conditioning requires. The coated glass oversails the floor level to create an unbroken surface that reduces the apparent depth of the floor plate when seen in reflection. The edge of the floor plate is cut away behind this oversailing portion and a combination of colour and reflective surface is inserted into the void created to 'bring the sky into the façade' when it is possible to see through the glass façade from the outside.

next page

Figure 17-22
WTC7 façade

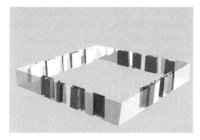

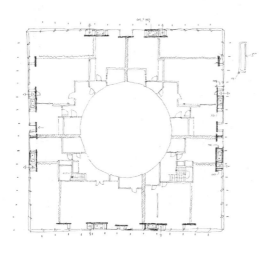
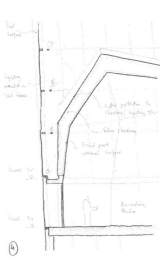

A second project for a façade was developed with Arup Facades for a residential building in Dublin's docklands. The Twisting Tower was won in competition and the Irish architects BCDH had again initially proposed double-skin facades which were rejected by the client for the same reasons as in the WTC7 building. The architects asked us to help them to maintain visual depth, a play of light, and a visual consistency within a single relatively thin wall zone with a high percentage (approximately 60%) of highly insulated and opaque panels. The problem was made more challenging by the twisting of the tower which either meant the panels had to twist themselves or have a complicated frame.

We initially produced a conceptual double-skin, producing a zone around the perimeter of the building which was used for a number of architectural, ventilation, and lighting uses, that gave depth to the façade but was also occupied space while providing the required percentage of highly insulated opaque panels. It also had the advantage of creating vertical exterior wall space in the interior of the flats to counter the rather unsettling effect of the tilted and angled mullions of the true exterior of the building.

The exterior appearance of the panels of the building went through several transformations and the final attempt to unify the exterior appearance of the building produced a new solution, which combines solar shading in some of the 'window' panels with a moiré effect within the shadow boxes of some of the opaque panels, to give a reading to the building which works at a variety of scales – an overall surface of white, a moiré pattern of the colour on the back of the white stripes, reflected in the back panel of the shadow box, and

previous page

Figure 23-32
Twisted Tower (U2 Tower)
Docklands, Dublin
Building architect: BurdonCraig
Dunne Henry, Dublin | Facade
Engineer: Arup Facade Engineering, London
2005-

Figure 33-43
Chapel for the Salvation Army |
101 Queen Victoria Street, London
| Building architect: Sheppard
Robson, London | Engineer: Ove
Arup & Partners, London
2002 - 2004

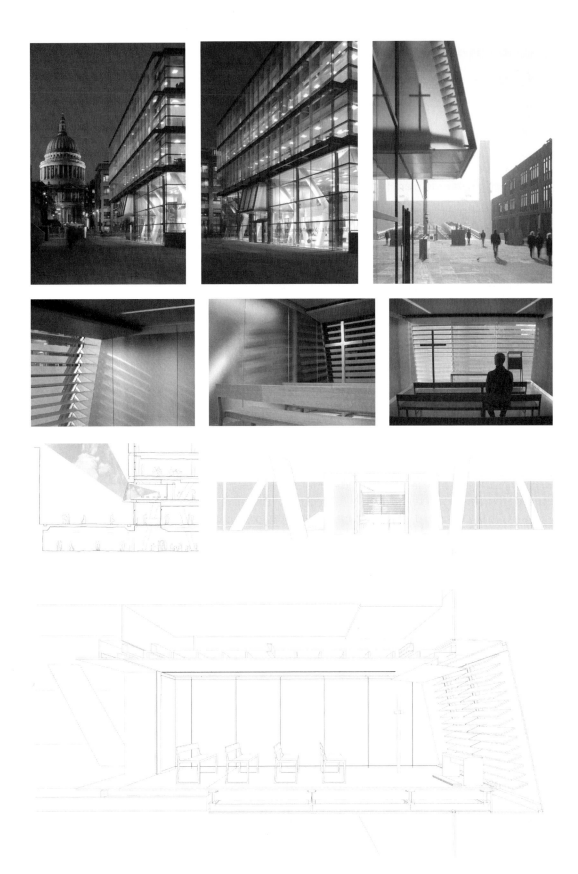

the detail of the stripes again when seen close to. It also integrated the 'sail' at the top of the building which extended beyond the building enclosure to give a clean silhouette to the top two floors, while shielding the outdoor spaces of the recording studios for U2.

4.   Unique situations:

The previous two examples were developed when the pressures on the space of the façade were high, but they connect in their visual language to more unusual types of envelope or screen which have been developed for unique situations.

Using the full possibilities of translucency, we have recently worked on the design of a chapel at the Salvation Army Headquarters in London. We were given this section of the building to develop by the building architects Sheppard Robson and its location and scale were pre-determined in their design: the small chapel for twenty people was placed projecting over the entrance to the building and the public footpath between St. Paul's Cathedral and the Thames. The Salvation Army wanted their faith to be at the heart of their headquarters, to be visible as such, but also to be private. We proposed a double-skinned wall, with a strongly flame-coloured interior wall as a metaphor for the strength of their belief, to glow through a simple clear translucent exterior skin that would shield the occupants from view. The double translucent wall would also serve to conceal the structure and the constant shift of shadows of people inside the space and the structure within the walls is manifested on the glass surfaces. The street wall of the chapel is clear and a series of semi-reflective louvers redirect the image of the sky overhead into the chapel as a backdrop for contemplation; bringing the image of the natural world into the space. As well as containing the structure, the void between the two walls is used as a duct for the air required to keep the single-glazed front façade free of condensation, and the air is re-circulated through the perforations of the timber acoustic ceiling. The image of the sky is intended to connect the busy worker at the very heart of the city to the environment in real time: this view can be interpreted simultaneously as a view toward heaven but also simply as a reminder of the presence of the ever-changing sky overhead; the 'everyday'.

The two-sided printed interlayer proposed in Dublin which we have been developing with manufacturers in the US has also recently been used for some interior screens used at the boundary between landside and airside areas in Terminal 5 at Heathrow Airport which is due to open in March 2008. The 'canyons' are the passages that the passengers must pass through, and through which they can't return: there are two only, each thirty metres long and fifteen metres wide. Security staff sometimes observe passengers from one very small room be-

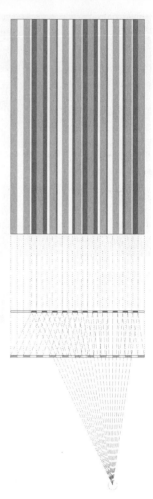

Fig 44-52
Heathrow screens

side this passage but it was felt that the typical 'mirror window' was too distinct and visually disruptive, so we took the semi-reflective glass used in the window as the basis for a treatment of the length of all the wall surfaces, that would simultaneously express the transition from land to air. A second surface of glass is placed in front of the semi-reflective 'one-way mirror', which has a special pattern printed onto it. The passenger sees vertical white stripes and, between them, the reflection of the coloured back of the stripes in the one-way mirror. The colour on the back of the stripe is different on each of the 27 panels along the length of the passage and so the moiré pattern of vertical bars appears to float beyond the white stripes and to change colour as the passenger progresses. The security personnel see adequately through the semi-reflective surface and between the stripes, and the exact position of their room is invisible.

A very different type of façade is developed at the base of the tower of the WTC7 where the conditions are quite unique. The lowest eight floors of the tower are occupied by the electrical transformers for lower Manhattan, and are concealed behind a blast-proof solid concrete façade whose only perforations are for ventilation. The vertical core of the building penetrates this base to connect the ground level to the office floors above. The task then, is to animate this façade and to make a coherent composition with the rest of the building. The conceptual connection of the component parts of the building is through the idea of a 'block of light', implied in the treatment of the lobby area and reiterated at the top of the building. The façade is animated by both daylight and artificial light. A vertical stainless steel grille of extruded triangular sections is used in panels, with the triangles welded at different angles in each panel, creating a surface of rich lustre, that catches the light in the surroundings from a variety of different angles. This façade constantly shifts in character reflecting either the deep shadow or intense sunlight of the environment around.

The façade is in fact composed of two layers of screens, each composed of different sized elements to minimize the moiré effect that we deliberately used at Heathrow. The lighting at night is a series of vertical blue/white LED strips concealed from direct view behind the frame support elements and shining into the void between the two layers of screen. They can be configured into a number of different of lighting scenarios but the most interesting was developed by Marek Walczak who used to work for JCDA in New York but now has his own interactive artwork company called Kinecity. The lights can be linked to a series of cameras on the outside of the building that register the movement of people on the pavement and turn on the lights only in the vertical band immediately in front of the pedestrian, as if to light their way. Thus, each person has their own 'guide', projected in eight-storey-high bars of light.

Fig 53-62
WTC7 base lighting

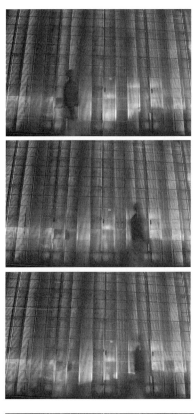

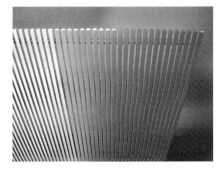

5.   Synthesis?

The envelope of the building is a permeable skin, though in the above examples it is restricted to the perimeter even if that boundary is broadened in some cases. In the last project, developed by JCDA in New York in collaboration with Matthias Schuler of Transsolar and the building architect Vince James, a different approach was taken. The Tulane University Students Centre is located in New Orleans, which has a very warm and humid climate. The early architecture of New Orleans took advantage of shading and cooling breezes to modulate the extremes of temperature and it was decided to use these precedents as a starting point to develop a design in which the building and envelope are inseperable; where the envelope becomes the building.

A heterogeneous membrane is wrapped around the pre-existing core, and is made more or less permeable depending on the environmental conditions outside and the uses of the spaces inside. The ground floor common room may be fully opened up by the use of vertically sliding 2.7m high glass window walls, and sliding/folding glass walls. (63)

Large pivoting glass windows ventilate the ballroom on the first floor. (64)

Lightweight canopies in perforated metal protect the southwestern and northeastern facades of the building and vertical louvres in a combination of timber and aluminium shield the southeastern façade. (65)

Large ceiling circular ceiling fans integrated into cylinders of translucent glass exploit the stack effect to ventilate the ballroom space, while pendulum fans elsewhere in the space force water across the surface of water walls to dehumidify the space. (66)

All of this adds up to a building where the whole perimeter of the space is variable and the ideal of opening up the building to the exterior that is reduced to its most banal by the simple expedient of large areas of flat glass, is followed through and becomes a well tempered, controlled and civilized structure that can be orchestrated and tuned to work in harmony with its environment. (67)

6.   Conclusion:

This small sample of some of the mutations of the envelope shows the range within the species is so vast that a new taxonomy may be necessary. The imperitives that guide the development from a cultural perspective may however be consistent, or at least not too divergent, even though the financial, climatic and social contexts from which

Figure 63-67
Tulane University Students Centre

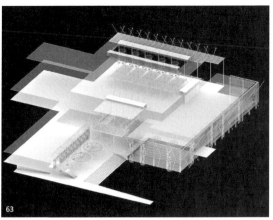

63

64

65

66

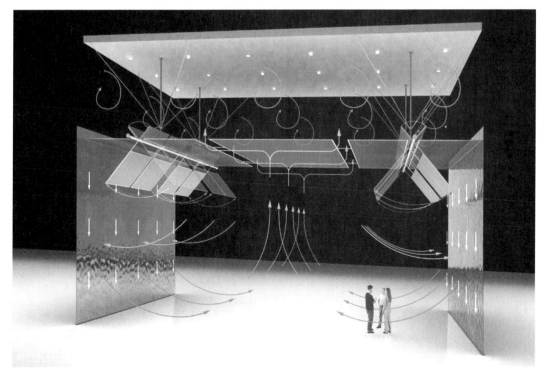

these examples have grown vary so enormously. Our works have in common the desire to connect the ordinary users to the natural forces in their environment and the natural world in as positive a way as possible, and to try to create a sense of wonder and awe at the potential beauty of the world.

This aspiration has to be developed in a cultural context that includes the prevailing construction methods, whatever they may be, from mass-production of curtain walling to more bespoke methods. To be able to develop the simplest of concepts one has to have a thorough understanding and control of the technical aspects of design and fabrication - a kind of 'broad specialism' – but this knowledge has to be guided by a design concept.

As I said: the future is unpredictable. It is clear however, that the fundamental positivistic assumption that we can all agree on a future model and work together to achieve it, evolved within a long established cultural climate that included economic expansion underpinned by expanding energy supplies, which cannot be assumed to be the case in the future. This is a huge shift, the implications of which have hardly begun to be grasped. It might be possible however, that this new situation coupled with our developing understanding of the interaction of complex systems and a respect for our place within the ecologies of the world, will present us with the opportunity to develop an architecture that incorporates an understanding of the environment, at both the functional, and the experiential level. The aspiration is to move toward a mature resolution of our relationship to our context, not just on the dry level of efficiency and the use of resources, but emotionally, symbolically and perceptually.

The Future Envelope is not conceivable without a direct and strong contribution to the climate concept of the entire building. Climate design is one of the younger disciplines that relate to façade construction, implementing environmental aspects.

Dipl.-Ing. Thomas Auer as principle of his company Transsolar, has been involved in this subject matter for over 20 years. His projects are astonishing examples of how the performance of facades can be tailored to the requirements for energy consumption and comfort.

The Future Envelope 1 – A Multidisciplinary Approach. U. Knaack and T. Klein (Eds.). IOS Press, 2008.

PERFORMANCE AS A GOAL
INTEGRATION AS THE APPROACH?

Thomas Auer

Transsolar

1.   Introduction

A building's energy performance, as well as user comfort and well-being, is mainly determined by the facade. This is becoming more and more important as people are starting to recognize how important daylight is for their well-being, and therefore their productivity. Studies in the US and Canada showed an increase in productivity and effectiveness in offices and schools of more than 10%. As important as daylight is the ability to adapt the facade to different climate conditions and indoor requirements. Glare and solar control, natural ventilation, and comfortable heating and cooling become more and more the driving parameters for highly efficient buildings (dynamic buildings).

The following parameters have a major impact on the energy performance and user comfort of a building:

- Heat losses
- Solar heat gains in summer
- Air tightness
- Daylight transmission and distribution
- Operable windows for natural ventilation

In the '90s there was a trend in central Europe to achieve dynamic buildings with layering. Every function was put into a specific layer, such as double facades with integrated shading devices and added daylight enhancement systems. Since it was a primary goal to take advantage of certain climate conditions to support building operation, the integration of mechanical components into the facade was an obvious conclusion. On one hand, this approach should ensure that the interaction between inside and outside "communicates" with the mechanical systems. On the other hand, having the main mechanical systems integrated in the facade optimizes flexibility. No installation is dedicated to the ceiling and internal walls, therefore walls could basically be anywhere.

Even as things become more and more integrated, all systems

are still applied as layers, and distribution systems (piping, duct-work, etc) are still independent of the facade. The future envelope consequently integrates all functions and becomes one piece. Energy generation will be added to the described functions. Photovoltaic and/or thermal solar collectors on the outer surface will feed power and hot water into the building systems. The integration of translucent insulation combined with phase change material on the inside creates a highly improved Trombe wall.

It becomes clear that integration instead of layering will provide endless opportunities.

2. History

The invention of the curtain wall and air-conditioning changed the traditional building culture towards more energy consumption and less user comfort. Figure 1 shows Manhattan in 1920 and today. In 1920 – without air conditioning – shading and operable windows as well as heavy, massive buildings were mandatory in order to survive in a climate like the East Cost of the US. The invention of air conditioning was essentially a prerequisite for the curtain wall.

Figure 1
Manhattan 1920 and today

This comparison certainly raises the question whether the invention of the curtain as well as modernism in general is going in the right direction. In the beginning of the modernism movement, issues like local climate conditions were entirely ignored.

Figure 2 shows Crown Hall, done by Mies van der Rohe and the Dayley Center, done by C.F. Murphy. Both buildings are considered as icons of modernism. Both buildings are fully glazed (single-layer) without shading. While Crown Hall has operable flaps at the bottom of the facade, it was at the time common – and is still common – to build buildings without operable windows and natural ventilation. The consequence is an enormous energy consumption on one side, and unacceptable comfort conditions on the other side, such as:

- Downdraft and low radiative temperature caused by the cold inner surfaces in winter.
- High radiative temperatures in summer.
- Draft and noise caused by the air conditioning.

Figure 2
Crown Hall and the Dayley Center in Chicago

3. High Performance glass buildings

Compared to the where it was at beginning of modernism, the performance of glass increased almost by an order of magnitude. Glass certainly became a high-tech product. Multiple glass layers, low-e and selective coatings, gas filling and fritting became common technologies in order to tailor the glass – based on specific requirements and – of course - budget.

Figure 3
Prisma Building, Frankfurt, using double facade technology

Buildings like the Prisma Building in Frankfurt, done by Auer, Weber and Partners have been a demonstration in terms of performance. The controlled double facade provides a thermal buffer in winter

and a pre-conditioning of supply air. In summer the double facade acts as a solar chimney to draw exhaust air out and protect the shading device inside the facade cavity. In conjunction with an inner atrium, the double facade provides for year-round natural ventilation.

The glass house "R 128" by Werner Sobek uses heat mirror glazing, where foils inside the glass create additional cavities. Photovoltaics on the roof operate a heat pump which provide heating and cooling. To achieve the performance levels required for a zero-energy building, 2 foils were necessary. The thermal resistance of the glass is comparable to an insulated wall.

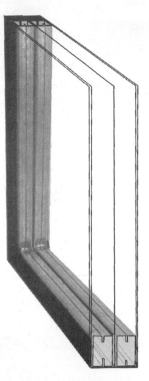

Figure 4
House R 128, Stuttgart, Germany with heat mirror glass

4.   Integration of mechanical equipment

The headquarters of Deutsche Post in Bonn, done by Murphy Jahn Architects, was one of the first major buildings using decentralized ventilation technology attached to the facade. Every single office essentially has its own air handling system, located in the raised floor (see Figure 5).

Air intake is from a double facade corridor. The unit provides fresh air heating and cooling. In addition, people can open the windows for natural ventilation.

opposite page

Figure 5
Decentralized ventilation box installed in the raised floor

Due to the decentralized system, the tower has no vertical air distribution, which also made the system economically viable.

Meanwhile, facade system manufacturers, such as Wicona and Schüco, provide facade systems with integrated mechanical systems (see Figure 6). It is certainly reasonable to merge the facade together with mechanical tools for the following reasons:

- Combination of the two systems which are the interface between inside and outside.
- One integrated control system for both systems.
- Industrial pre-fabrication of these high tech products which determine the building's performance.

Figure 6
Wicona TEmotion facade with integrated mechanical systems

5. Future Systems

Using smart materials such as translucent insulation, glass-fiber reinforced concrete, phase change materials, etc., provide endless possibilities to tailor the facade performance. At the same time, the facade becomes a load-bearing wall. Bi-metal inlets provide shading in summer. Integrated capillary mats provide radiant heating and cooling. Additional elements for energy generation such as photovoltaic or thermal solar panels can also be integrated.

In an ideal world, the house will be based on three elements: superstructure, facade and fit-out.

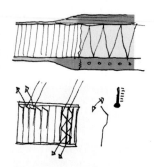

Figure 7
Graded wall principles
(Marcel Bilow)

The multidisciplinary approach serves numerous goals. It is not only mandatory to fulfill the requirements of such a complex topic as facade construction with its many participants from various disciplines, but is also the basis for a multifaceted search for new strategies and approachs.

Prof. Dr.-Ing. Holger Techen's work is a good example of why structural design not only serves as the means to realize projects, but, as part of many, is an essential step for the entire process. The structural engineers's knowledge and capability is highly important for the final product.

The Future Envelope 1 – A Multidisciplinary Approach. U. Knaack and T. Klein (Eds.). IOS Press, 2008.

FUTURE ENVELOPES FROM IMAGINATION TO REALIZATION

Holger Techen

Institute for structural design
University for applied sciences
Frankfurt/Main

1.   Summary / Introduction

The future envelope – we have already begun searching for answers to the question of where this development will lead us. Already today there are many projects all over the world that display the step-by-step development of the facade. Each of these 'unusual' projects highlights the trends of tomorrow's building envelope.

The goal should be to analyze these projects and to derive meaningful research and development tasks from the results. In doing this, the focus may not be on the design idea alone, but needs to encompass the realization of the design concept into a real building.

This article will demonstrate this process highlighted by two projects. In both cases there was a clearly defined design approach by the architect.

Based on my earlier field of activity as primarily responsible project managing engineer with the engineering firm Ingenieurbüro Bollinger + Grohmann, I will introduce two projects with high potential for innovation to demonstrate the process from initial design idea to realization.

2.   Zollverein School, Zeche Zollverein, Essen, Germany

The Zollverein School is based on an extremely stringent and minimal design approach by the architects SANAA from Tokyo (Fig. 1). This approach presupposes a new attitude of the individual design partners and the developer for the planning process. For an integrated design process, it is essential to meld the different contract subsections into one. In doing so, all participants need to understand and respect the needs of all other partners. This approach was first employed for the conception of steel reinforced concrete ceilings, by working out possibilities to use ceilings and other structurally relevant building components not only for load transfer but also as storage medium, for conduit and as space forming elements.

For the Zollverein School the team compared several ceiling variants using a rating matrix. From criteria such as surface quality, cost, manufacturing method and options to integrate building services, the steel reinforced concrete ceiling emerged as the optimum solution. With span widths of up to 16 m, displacement bodies were inserted into the 50 cm thick ceiling, resulting in a weight reduction of approximately 30%. Conduit for activated building components and smoke detectors were inserted underneath the displacement bodies (Fig. 2). Additionally, large built-in light fixtures were to be integrated in a regular grid. In order to meet the wish for a seamless fair faced concrete ceiling, the ceiling needed to include a higher degree of reinforcement in the lower reinforcement layer to limit

Figure 1
Design model

crack widths. Due to the ceiling fixtures also being integrated in the ceiling, this led to finely adjusted laying and assembly methods.

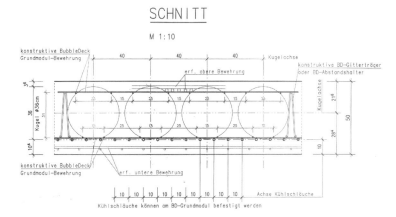

SCHNITT

M 1:10

Figure 2
Sectional view of the ceiling with the position of the displacement bodies and activated building components

This high degree of interdisciplinary design coordination also resulted in increased tendering and awarding efforts, because numerous contract subsections for building services had to be tendered in advance together with the structural works.

During the course of the contract negotiations it was important to clearly define dependencies and responsibilities between the structural works and the herein integrated building services planning (Fig. 3+4).

Figure 3
Lower reinforcement layer, piping for activated building components, displacement bodies, built-in light fixtures

Figure 4
Arrangement of high-load posts

The connection of the glass dividing walls on the office level stood out as a very significant design issue. They were to span from floor to ceiling without visible fixtures. It was, therefore, necessary to include a regular grid of 7 cm deep and 6 cm wide grooves in the fair faced concrete ceiling to accommodate the mounting fixtures for the upper edge of the glass panels (Fig. 5). As a result the ceiling was allocated an additional function as a space-shaping element.

Figure 5
Glass dividing walls with concealed mounting brackets

The weight reduction by means of displacement bodies had specific design-related impact on the load transfer to the core elements, the bond columns and the external walls. SANAA's architectural approach for the exterior walls was a thin exterior skin.

Realizing the exterior walls in form of typical double-skin fair faced concrete walls with core insulation would have resulted in walls of 50 cm thickness. Alternative measures, such as adding mineral plaster as interior or exterior insulation, would have contradicted the design approach on a fundamental level.

The variant used in this project is based on an idea by the building services planner. The concept of the so-called 'active thermal insulation' calls for heating the exterior concrete walls. Water is heated to 27° via a heat exchanger and is then circulated in tubing set in concrete.

Large volumes of mine water with a temperature of approximately 30°C are continuously pumped from a depth of about 1000 m on the colliery grounds near the building's location to prevent the earth from rising. Part of the mine water now flows through a heat exchanger, designed specifically for this purpose, which heats the water in the closed-loop circulation tubing within the exterior walls. However, the heating of the exterior walls does not serve as a heating system, but should be considered as an equivalent passive measure of thermal insulation.

The ecobalance of this approach results in a significant reduction of CO_2 output compared to conventional thermal insulation.

In comparison to a fair faced concrete wall with core insulation that would have had a total thickness of 50 cm due to structural and energetic requirements, the integration of 'active thermal insulation' reduced the wall thickness of the exterior walls to 30 cm.

In addition, by eliminating the need for formwork for a double-skin exterior wall the manufacturing cost and construction time were reduced significantly.

The architectural approach of a seamless concrete cube created challenges related to the structural construction of the exterior walls. Comprehensive research was necessary to illustrate the various types of stress caused by temperature changes in the exterior walls in a realistic manner. The unique arrangement of the window openings called for careful consideration of load transfer - considering the walls being only 30 cm thick but 10.50 m high. (Fig. 6)

Figure 6
Second floor exterior wall with a free-standing wall during the building process

The coordination process among architecture, building services and load-bearing structure, already complex when planning the ceilings, increased further during the advanced planning stages of the exterior walls. Manufacturing methods needed to be coordinated with the optimum conduit for the 'active thermal insulation' and the formwork (Fig. 7+8).

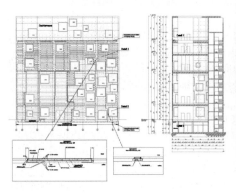 

During a continuative, iterative process, the positions of the window openings were coordinated with the piping network, structural stress, configuration of reinforcement and other conduits. From an architectural point of view it was important to construct a continuous formwork, avoiding seams at story-level. This required early discussions with formwork manufacturers so that solutions that would not exceed the budget could be included during the early planning stages (Fig. 9)

Figure 7
Key plan of the conduit for the active thermal insulation (office Winter)

Figure 8
Installation of the conduit for the active thermal insulation

Figure 9
Building upon completion

3.   Coffee house Lichtblick 360°, Innsbruck, Austria

The architecture firm Dominique Perrault planned a fully glazed pavilion, which was built on the roof of the Rathaus Passage in Innsbruck.

This pavilion, used as a coffee house and bar, comprises a filigree transparent structure. The building has a cylindrical shape with a diameter of approximately 9.35 m and a height of 3.60 m (Fig. 10).

Figure 10
The architect's design idea of the fully glazed building envelope

The design is based on clearly structured building components. A membrane fixed in a clamping ring serves as the roof. The pretension is mounted on an off-center point in the building with downward tension. The resulting funnel shape is created by the elastic deformation of the material. The lowest point comprises the drainage opening.

The membrane is mounted to the edge beam by means of welt seams and aluminum clamping bars. At the lowest point, the membrane is clamped with aluminum rings into which a vertical pulling force is introduced to provide pretension (Fig. 11)

Figure 11
Lifting of the pre-tensioned membrane

The outer pressure ring is constructed in the form of a steel gird-er which, besides structural functions, also accommodates building services functions. The box girder lies on 12 curved glass panels. The middle tension device of the membrane is realized with glass pres-sure springs. The spring force introduced corresponds to a weight-loading of 800 kg. Adjustment of this force produces a membrane pretension that guarantees the dimensional stability of the mem-brane even under water and snow loads, so that the drainage area remains at the lowest point and the formation of water sacks are avoided (Fig. 12).

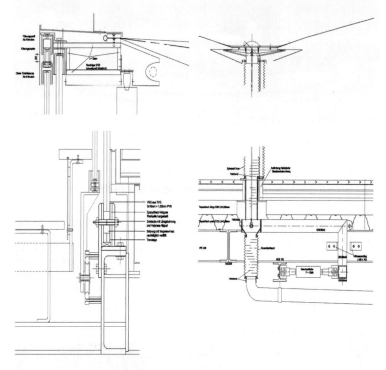

Figure 12
Details of membrane mounts

The base of the curved glass panels are clamped into a continuous steel ring which is screwed to the steel girder grid. The girder grid is built on the existing concrete ceiling of the Rathaus Passage, sit-ting on 8 supporting points. To compensate for the tolerances be-tween the steel structure and the curved glass panels, the LSG glass panels are cast in the curved steel section with permanently elastic epoxy resin (Fig. 13).

The vertical and horizontal load transfer of the entire building is con-ducted exclusively through the curved LSG panels. The curved shape provide the glass panels with sufficient stability to transfer the verti-cal loads. Horizontal stiffening, which needed to be specified for ex-treme wind speeds of up to 150 km/h as well as earthquakes, is carried out solely by the circularly arranged panels. During dimensioning and the approval process various failure scenarios were examined, which replaced building component tests.

In addition to the global examinations it was important to develop connection details for this novel structure that complied with the materials and construction methods used. These developments were conducted in a close partnership between the architect and the engineer. Coordination with the executing company required frequent presence at the construction site and, before that, for the preparation for the glass elements (Fig. 14).

Figure 13
Assembly and test loading of the membrane roof on the free-standing glass panels

Figure 14
Coffee house upon completion

4. Summary

These two projects show that for load-bearing components with cross functions, it is particularly important to intensively monitor the concepts developed by design team during the execution phase and to motivate the executing companies with these innovative approaches so that the design ideas can be realized as close to the original approach as possible.

As an architect, façade planner and researcher in the field of façades, **Dipl.-Ing. Tillmann Klein** looks at ways to innovate façade construction. The paper focuses on opportunities to introduce more complexly engineered integrated components and the possible effects on the building industry and the design process.

The Future Envelope 1 – A Multidisciplinary Approach. U. Knaack and T. Klein (Eds.). IOS Press, 2008.

EVOLUTION OR REVOLUTION OF SYSTEMS IN FAÇADE TECHNOLOGY

Is Function Integration the Strategy for the Future?

Tillmann Klein

Leader Facades Research
Group
Faculty of Architecture
Delft University of Technology

Abstract

The metal-glass façade has almost reached its final development stage.

A trend for integrated design solutions for new façade concepts can be observed. This paper illustrates examples and describes the characteristics of function integration. It focuses on the strategic possibilities of function integration for the development of the future metal-glass façade and describes the results on the physical façade construction and on the design and building process.

Keywords: Facade construction, Function integration, Systemized solutions, Standards, Design collaboration

1. Introduction

The process of building façades has a long tradition. It is subjected to cultural issues and to established methods of design contracting and building industries.

The particularity of facade construction compared to other disciplines lies, amongst others, in the relatively low number of repetitions and, considering the value of the finished product, rather low financial capacities of the parties involved.

This has led to rather conservative attitudes in terms of invention. New demands stemming from the thought of sustainability and energy savings and new developments in materials science show the need and the potential for a different approach in engineering and production techniques for building façades.

This paper will focus on the metal-glass façade, which, as a relatively young product (60 to 80 years is young for a building product), proves to be one of the most successful products in the façade industry. The characteristics of this type of facade have led to a broad acceptance within the architectural world. The desire for transparency and lightness and the concept of separating the façade from the load-bearing structure of the building was and remains to be very successful. In principle, its modular structure can be adapted easily and therefore it offers a relatively great freedom of design.

The development of the metal-glass façade has undergone several steps. With the advent of aluminum extrusion, aluminum-glass facades have taken precedence over steel-glass structures. And since the eighties and nineties, energy performance has increased in importance and caused new developments in the field of high-performance sealing methods. However, the basic principle of construction has remained the same. The metal-glass façade has almost reached its final development stage.

Metal-glass facades are a good example for highly systemized products as a reaction to the needs of the building market.

Figure 1
Crown Hall, Illinois Institute of Technology, Chicago, Ludwig Mies van der Rohe, 1956

Figure 2
Crown Hall, Illinois Institute of Technology, Chicago, Detail of façade

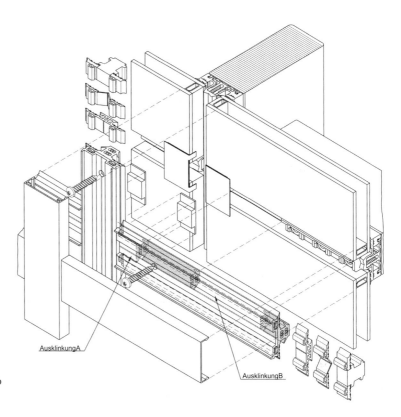

Figure 3
Detail of post-beam system, Raico
Bautechnic

AusklinkungA

AusklinkungB

2. Design Collaboration and Standards

A high degree of individuality is the one factor that most of the realized façade projects have in common. Architectural design takes the front seat, and the design team has to find ways to realize it. Typically, this team varies from project to project as do the companies that execute the construction. The number of team members participating in any given project has increased over the years. The architect as an integrator relies on the collaboration of building services engineers, climate designers, structural engineers, facade designers, and project leaders as well as representatives of system manufacturers and executing companies. They decide on a case by case basis how much or how little innovation will be introduced into the product.

The result is a highly individual façade product based on known system technologies. The design team is obligated to adhere to current building laws and norms. System suppliers have reacted to this requirement. They are broken down to the system level. Such systems are tested for wind proofing and u-values etc. in certain configurations. Since the invention of the metal-glass façade, they have undergone continuous specialization and have developed into mature products. Adopting the systems to the particular circumstance is an integral part of the design process.

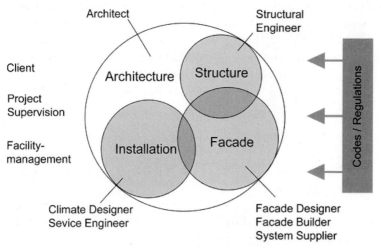

Figure 4
Design collaboration. Varying design teams from project to project

The number of projects being realized with technologies that are not standardized according to the facade industry is relatively low. This not only requires a courageous team, ready to carry great risk; but also calls for developers who are not afraid of experiments. The impact on the development of the future façade is, of course, very high.

Thus, systems are necessary to effectively manage a project. However, one inherent characteristic of systems is the sluggishness in terms of innovations. They always constitute the limitation of freedom, since a fundamental changeability of highly technological systems is hard to achieve. Exemplary for this problem is the fact, that, over the last few years, metal-glass facades have only been improved marginally in terms of their heat insolating functionalities.

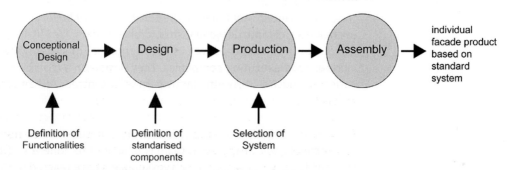

3. Façade Functionalities

Figure 5
Standars and systems in the design process

One key factor of developing structures lays in their functionality, i.e. their capability to fulfill certain functions. The following section describes in how far façade functions have influenced current structural systems.

The façade's traditional task is to separate the usable interior space from the uncontrollable exterior climate. The entire façade structure has been developed over millennia to meet this basic demand. Rain and wind proofing, thermal separation, sun protection and security. The contact between interior and exterior space as well as the architectural design are, of course, other basic functions required from the façade.

The following structural elements can be derived:
- The construction of the facade and its relationship to the overall structure of the building as well as the interface with neighboring buildings.
- The integration of specialized components such as transparent elements to connect the interior and exterior space in the form of exchangeable infill elements.
- And sealing components.

When examining the developments of current facade concepts, we can see the trend to extend on the functions the building envelope fulfils.

There are several reasons for this tendency. For example, new demands that are stemming from the thought of sustainability and energy savings.

The façade's importance in terms of the building's architectural and urban appearance makes it an interesting element for the search for new ways of expression. It mirrors the degree of technology of the building process. Its function to separate the interior and exterior climates provides the façade with a high potential in terms of energy performance and user comfort.

These are a few examples of new facade functions:
- The integration of the facade into the technical concept of the building; meaning an active contribution to heating, cooling, ventilation. Ensuring maximum operating comfort for the user.
- Improved energy performance and energy gain.
- Adaptability to changing user requirements, meaning changeableness in terms of physical demands or even physical components such as transparency etc..
- Upgrade ability related to technical performance.

But also:
- Freedom of form and design as well as media functions for presentations and advertisements.

These new functions as well as others still unknown to us today will have to find their way into the facade structure. The traditional arrangement of functions within the physical façade space is either side-by-side, layered or a combination of both. A layered arrangement enables a combination of different functions, such as sun protection elements in front of glass surfaces, which can be added when necessary and regulate incoming energy and light. Functional separation also occurs within individual components. Special glazing consists of several layers of glass which can be enhanced with certain coatings, depending on the requirement. A façade section is divided into elements for structural loads, sealing, fixing of infilled components and an exterior cover cap for the design.

The separation of functions is a proven method, extending to the distribution of tasks to different subcontracts such as metal construction, electric and sanitary installations. In how far the separation of functions in façade construction has developed as a reaction to the conditions of the building industry is a different question. But it certainly has its specific advantages. The participating parties can focus on their specific discipline and can specialize further. The interface is such that it allows for independent developments of the individual components. It is a fact that the building industry has committed to the principle of function separation.

The following section will illustrate a few examples which depart from this principle.

Exemplary projects
The Facades Research Group has undertaken certain projects to research the integration of components.

Modular facade element
The goal of this mock-up was to create a facade element with an integrated decentralized air-conditioning unit as well as the use of fibre reinforced concrete as an alternative material for aluminum. The width of the fibre reinforced concrete sections is the same as those of the original aluminum sections and could even be smallerThe perforated grid symbolizes a building services module for the functions ventilating, heating and cooling, which, at the time, did not exist. Part of the element was built following the box window principle with wind proof sun protection. Another part was designed as a single-skin façade. Theoretically, these methods of construction can be determined freely and can therefore address the desired arrangement of the functions.

An insulation core was inserted in the continuous frame. The external glass surfaces were installed directly into the fibrated concrete frame with rubber strips, without the need for standard systems.

Figure 6
Modular façade element, Knaack, Bilow 2004. Glassfiber reinforced concrete with decentralized climate unit

Figure 7
Detail of modular façade element

Heating Panel

As part of his thesis, Marcel Bilow developed a concept for a façade heating panel. The principle of a traditional façade panel was modified such that a fibre reinforced concrete skin was mounted on the interior side instead of the typical sheet metal skin. This allows the insertion of capillary heat ducts. The function of the insulating component was enhanced to include the functions heating and cooling. At the same time, a thermal mass was generated that has a positive impact on the indoor climate. The component is designed such that it can be integrated into a standard post-and-beam façade. The concept also includes the connection of the water pipes.

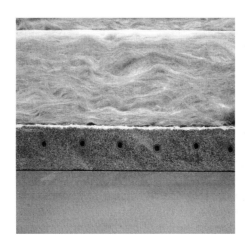

Figure 8
Function integrated façade panel

Figure 9
Section through panel

Jackbox

Recently, an advancement of this principle was realized with the Jackbox at the technical college FH-Lippe Höxter. The Jackbox is a multifunctional room object: light, modularly changeable and moveable. Its construction was based on methods used in the automotive industry. Here, large sandwich elements are used for trucks. On the interior side, fibre reinforced concrete with heating or cooling ducts are again used. In addition, it serves to provide the component with sufficient rigidity. The exterior FRP (fibre reinforced plasic) skin is bendable; so a bent shape can be generated by milling into the insulation core. The subsequently applied layer of fibre reinforced concrete freezes the shape. The structure is relatively light and forms the entire outer skin of the object. The edges of the skins are formed such that they can be joined into one another. There is no need for an additional joining element.

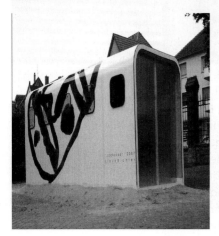 

Zollverein School of Management and Design

The basic principle of the facade comprises of a single-leaf-fair faced concrete wall with embedded looped warm water pipes. These pipes are 2 cm (0.8 in) in diameter and are spaced at intervals of 20 – 40 cm (8 – 16 in). They are filled with the warm mine water which serve as "active" heat insulation during winter. Thus, neither core insulation nor any other double-leaf structure is necessary. In addition to increased wall thickness alternative solutions would have required expansion joints in the outer shell to accommodate for thermal expansion.

The "active" thermal insulation concept allows for a construction method using concrete which is typically limited to more moderate climates: the inner and outer shell of the building is constructed from single-leaf concrete walls approximately 30 cm (12 in) thick. Within this concrete shell, looped heating ducts are embedded that are filled with warm mine water which regulate the indoor temperature as well as prevent frost on the exterior.

Figure 10
Jackbox, Multifunctional Project

Figure 11
Assembly of Jackbox

The irregularly placed windows were positioned according to the requirements of the indoor functions and mounted on the inner side of the concrete shell. Recesses are made in the surface to accommodate the aluminum frames. Rainwater is drained off on the interior side of the wall and the warm wall temperature prevents frost.

The quality of the fair-faced concrete surfaces reveals significant effort in terms of design and coordination as well as high-quality construction.

Figure 12
School of Management and Design, Essen, SANAA, Tokio with Heinrich Böll, Essen, 2006

5. The Revolution of the Standard through Function Integration

The question is whether we can revolutionize the facade structure from the inside out by applying the philosophy of function integration.

The benefit and the appeal of integrated solutions lie in their efficiency when adapting them to one or more functions. Potentially smaller high-performance components are possible. But the disadvantages are also obvious: Specialization makes it difficult to manufacture integrative components in an open and flexible manner. The effort is larger than with standardized solutions.

Moreover, integrative concepts have an impact on the design process. As previously described, the project teams face problems that increase in complexity. And this development also challenges the boundaries of traditional facade building and the building industry has to react to these requirements as well. The traditional methods of subcontracts such as metal construction, electric and sanitary installation reach their limits. If, for example, a heater is no longer simply installed in the interior side of the façade (and this already requires coordination between different subcontracts), but integrated into the actual façade structure, traditional boundaries and responsibilities for the individual components of the overall façade project become blurred. This is true for the design, the planning process and final warranty.

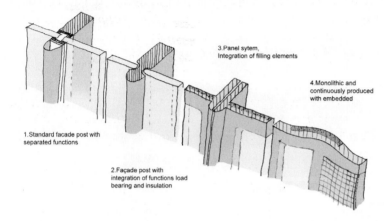

3.Panel sytem,
Integration of filling elements

4.Monolithic and
continuously produced
with embedded

1.Standard facade post with
separated functions

2.Façade post with
integration of functions load
bearing and insulation

Figure 13
Schematic development of the
standard façade post to a 'super
integrated façade'

6.   Conclusion

Under certain circumstances, the integration of functions makes sense; particularly if we are dealing with the development of highly specialized façade components.

However, the success of this philosophy depends on the following criteria:

Design and Engineering
- Architectural quality and acceptance by the deciding parties.
- Highly skilled design collaboration
- Capability and willingness of the manufacturing companies to get involved and to support the development.
- Intelligent conception of integrative components, measured by their adaptability to future façade functions such as upgradeability.

Production and Assembly
- Possibilities for new manufacturing methods that enable the production of integrative products and, at the same time, ensure adequate variability and flexibility. In this context, the potential of generative manufacturing methods such as rapid manufacturing are noteworthy.
- The façade manufacturers´skill level and the production facilities

Building Market
- Architectural quality of the façade product
Better performance than current philosophy of separation to compensate potentially higher development and building costs

Thus, we have to address the following topics:

- Definition of future functionalities required from a façade.
- Re-consideration of system standards in relationship with these functionalities, such as modularity, for example.
- Development of new manufacturing methods

Therefore, even if the redistribution of the tasks within the construction process proves to be successful; a certain degree of standardization of integrated concepts will always be necessary. Without standardization no façade product can be successful in the market.

References

Brookes, A. (1998). Cladding of Buildings, Spon, London

Eekhout, M. (1997). Popo of ontwerpmethoden voor bouwproducten en bouwcomponenten, Delft University Press, Delft

Halman, J.I.M, Hofer, A.P., Vuuren, W.van (2003) Plattform-Driven Development of Product Families: Linking Theory with Practice, Journal of Product Innovation Management, Vol. 20 pp149-162

Hausladen, G. (2005). Clima Design, Callway-Verlag, München

Herzog, T. (2004). Fassaden Atlas, Birkhäuser, Berlin

Knaack, U. (1998). Konstruktiver Glasbau, Rudolf Müller, Köln

Knaack,U., Klein,T (2005). Fassadenplanung mit Systemen, Deutsches Architektenblatt, Nr.12 pp 59-62

Knaack, U., Klein,T., Bilow, M., Auer, T. (2007) Fassaden- Prinzipien der Konstruktion, Birkhäuser, Berlin

Oesterle, R., (et al.) (1999). Doppelschalige Fassaden, Callway-Verlag, München

Ulrich,K. (1995) The role of product architecture in the manufacturing firm, Research Policy, Vol.24 pp 419-440

Dr. ir. Wim Poelman, as material specialist and product designer, focuses on strategies, methods and tools for the design process. In the field of industrial design, methodology plays a significantly role, whereas in architecture methodology, unfortunately, seems to be underestimated topic. This chapter gives a stimulating overview of the potential of this approach for the future facade. It offers the possibility to see the façade as what it actually is – an industrial product.

The Future Envelope 1 – A Multidisciplinary Approach. U. Knaack and T. Klein (Eds.). IOS Press, 2008.

THE FUTURE ENVELOPE AND DESIGN METHODOLOGY

Wim Poelman

Chair of Product Development
Faculty of Architecture
Delft University of Technology

Poelman + Partners

1. Introduction

Ye Hadi Teherani (2007), a German architect, claims that the architect must be a generalist in order to achieve good results. Of course he should be a generalist, but more than that an integralist. The difference between a generalist and a integralist is that a generalist knows something about everything while an integralist is able to make different disciplines work together. The specialism of the integralist is methodology and, with respect to methodology we can learn something from industrial designers. With respect to design solutions they cut of the edges and break down the problem. They would not start with the whole universe of architecture and society, but with conclusions of a concrete market study or with the definition of a technical problem. The industrial design approach could perhaps be the typical BT (building technology) approach versus the A (architecture) attitude.

How does new technology (and that is what we are really talking about) find the way into the future façade? Is it the ingenious approach of a generalist or a planned strategy of little steps? Should we look at architecture as an assembly of products?

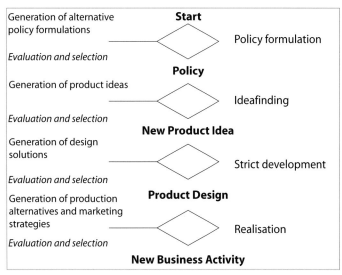

Figure 1
Roozenburg/Eekels (1995)

97

This was about the briefing for this presentation. It is regarded as an invitation to present some concepts for thinking about technology diffusion in architecture. Starting point is the, by industrial designers, frequently used model of Roozenburg/Eekels shown below. It is interesting to notice that Roozenburg/Eekels pay no explicit attention is given to the technology management aspect. In this model the technology plan is part of the policy formulation. However without having first thought about the product, it is impossible to define a policy about product technology. This could be solved by inserting a box between "policy formulation" and "idea finding", called "technology definition", but they did not.

2.   Integration of technology assessment in the design process

A key question in this context is how to integrate technology assessment into the design process. Literature on this subject is scarce, although there are a few publications which could be used for exploring the way technology assessment could be integrated.

Frost et al (1992) distinguish P thinking and S thinking (Problem definition and Solution definition). Frost argues that P thinking is also a creative activity, which is something most people fail to realize. Paying insufficient attention to p thinking leads, according to Frost, to problems later on in the design process. To be able to find and evaluate a technological solution, it is necessary to formulate the problem first.

Frost emphasizes the importance of problem definition, which may well be the key to an improved assessment of technological possibilities in the design process. Problem analysis is an underestimated, important phase in the design process. In most design projects in design schools with which the author was confronted, the "problem analysis" was poorly worked out. Mostly, the students jumped straight from the acquisition of information to the list of demands. A test with PhD students in advanced engineering yielded the conclusion that they were not able to analyze a relatively simple function like a door closer. They were unable to let go of the product itself sufficiently in order to analyze the functions, which take place in the context of a door. In the domain of information technology, the design of flow charts is necessary to be able to write a program. Products outside this domain seem simple, but they are not. There is some reason to assume that more attention to function analysis could result in:

- Human values related to a product function
- More insight into what the demands for technological solutions

are
- More insight into the side effects of technological solutions.

For finding an answer to this problems we should go back to the fundamentals of design as presented in figure 2.

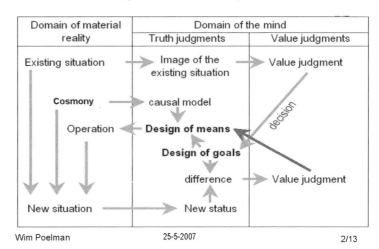

Wim Poelman   25-5-2007   2/13

Figure 2
Fundamentals of design

In the design process two domains interact with each other, the domain of material reality and the domain of the mind. Within the domain of the mind two judgments are distinguished: the judgment of truth and the judgment of value.

Say an architect has the chance to develop a complete new façade. There is an existing situation in which there are a lot of realized façade-systems, there is a specific situation for the façade to build, there is a lot of technology available and many people have just as many opinions about facades.

In the domain of the architects mind there is a lot of knowledge of which he thinks it's true or not. Architects not always believe in the same things. Even if he believes that things are true, it does not mean that he judges it as important. The judgment of architects about technology, society, design etc.. may differ very much.

Nevertheless, his judgment is the most important input for a design of "goals". He/she will not be aware of the fact that he/she is designing goals, but he does. The design of goals can be packed in a program of demands (like industrial designers do), design specifications or in a list of functionalities. It can also be just in his mind or in minutes of a meeting. The problem is that the design of goals is ill-documented most of the times, which will have a direct influence on the success of the façade. Even if the "design of means" is excellent.

To be able to realize a "design of means" of a facade it is necessary to start from a so-called "causal model". A causal model provides information how aspects are related to each other. A causal model of a façade will be much more complex then a causal model of a Philips shaver. Many parameters determine the functioning of a façade. To mention some: wind, rain, temperature, building construction, human behavior inside, urban environment, view of stakeholders with respect to beauty, available budgets, capabilities of suppliers, trees in the neighborhood, etc..

In general, architects do not have a complete causal model to their disposal when designing a façade. The only possibility is to design on basis of so-called "partial rationality". They think they took all aspects in consideration, but they did not. We cannot blame them, because they are not specialists in building up abstract models for a design concept. System engineers are, but they mostly are invited after a design of means is proposed.

Information for setting up the causal model comes from the domain of reality. The term cosmony is used by design scientists (e.g. Eekels/Roozenburg) for the coherence of reality. When a designer does not have knowledge about how the domain of reality functions, it is impossible to derive a causal model from it for a certain design of goals.

The rest of the figure will speak for itself. A design will change reality. This change will be judged and this judgment may lead to a new design of means, maybe for the next building.

The concept of a distinction between design of goals and design of means is in line with the difference which Frost makes between P(problem)-thinking and S(solution)-thinking. P-thinking leads to design of goals and S-thinking to design of means. Frost found out that designers tend to S-thinking more then to P-thinking, at the cost of innovation. Van den Kroonenberg was one of the first professors in the Netherlands who paid attention to P-thinking (Methodic Design). However his starting point was always a technical problem. Non-technical problems are more difficult to analyze. In non-technical problems we, as designers, are dependent on psychologists, sociologists, etc..

An interesting proposition is that most successful innovation result from a new design of goals, rather than a new design of means. A famous example is the Walkman. In fact the design of means already existed. A small tape recorder with earphones was already used in museums for guidance of people. Sony design a new goal: listening to music in trains, on bicycles and everywhere.

It would be interesting to see I new goals could be designed with a façade as a starting point.

3.   The funnel model

The funnel model of Muller (figure 3) is directly in line with the reflections above. With the design of goals as a starting point it the design process starts with the design of a basic structure. In the basic structure the functions which come out of the design of goals are organized and distributed over functional subsystems.

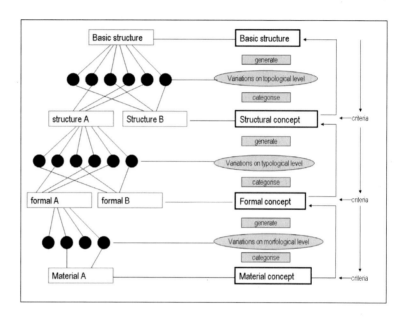

Figure 3
The funnel model

The next step is a structural concept in which dimensions are added to the schematic basic structure. Here we will see that many options are possible. Criteria in your design of goals will help to select one or more preferred options.

The next step is to study the potential of chosen structural concepts for designing concepts on formal level. Here the form giving skills of the architect come in. Many concepts could be the outcome of this phase and also for this selection the criteria will be indispensable.

The last phase is the materialization of the chosen concept.

There is some criticism on this model because of the material selection, which takes place at the end of the process. This criticism is not justified, simply because of the fact that material choice may be part of the design of goals. Analysis of cosmony could result in a goal to design a façade in e.g. pultrusion profiles. A reason could be that the potential of this technology is not researched yet, or that it is necessary to present something really new. The fact that Audi has chosen for aluminum has nothing to do with their design of means. It is a matter of design of goals, resulting from marketing.

The diffusion of new technology in architecture is not just related to design. It is however related to product development (the name of the chair). And product development needs disciplines like marketing and technology assessment.

4. Deficiencies in technology assessment capabilities

Durrani et al (1998) argues that there are some important weaknesses with respect to the technology assessment function in companies:

- Lack of integration between market needs, product attributes and technology availability;
- Weak mechanism to support and formalize technology acquisition and related decision making.
- Lack of integration between technology acquisition and product development processes.

The first argument refers to the question of market-pull and technology-push. Technologists know what is possible, but know little about market needs. The marketers know all about market needs, but know very little about what is possible from a technological point of view. Without communication, neither would be able to think up new product attributes on the basis of new technology. Communication, however, is difficult because of a 'cultural gap' and difference in jargon. The architect probably functions as a middleman between the principle and the technologists.

The technology acquisition problem has also been discussed before. Often, there is no technology plan, not to mention defined monitoring tasks. Analyzing interesting technology domains by using 'technology trees' (Butter 1989) is a useful tool, which is seldom applied. Nor is technological network-building something that management is prepared to spend a great deal of attention on. Although some improvement has occurred, the integration of technology acquisition and product development is still deficient. In many cases, the initiatives for new technological developments come from research. Architecture thus becomes an "end of pipe" activity that is intended to integrate the previously made technological choices. The designer's task is in that case limited to making technology 'usable'. Large companies, especially those manufacturing consumer products, passed that stage some time ago, and in many cases today start with the user.

5. Utility, functionality and usability

One such company has developed an approach in which a distinction is made between "utility", "functionality" and "usability" (Rakers, 1990). These three aspects subsequently prompt three key questions.

Utility: What should the product do for the user?
Functionality: How can this be realized from a technical point of view?
Usability: How can we ensure that users can handle the technology?

In fact, these three questions are eminently characteristic of the profession of architecture. Every designer should first go back to the aspect of utility. After this complex matter has been explored, the question of functionality arises. At this point, the inventory and assessment of technological opportunities takes place. Making an inventory of technology implies the availability of information. An awareness of the technological potency must be present before the start of the project.

These leads should be standing by in this process. In the majority of cases, realizing the functionality will not be the responsibility of the architect, but of specialists, such as mechanical engineers, microelectronics specialists etcetera. Usability, however, is a direct responsibility of the architect. Because of the general demands connected with "design for all" and the possibilities to develop intelligent products, this responsibility implies specialist knowledge about anthropometrical as well as about informational ergonomics.

6. Methodology for technology assessment

An integrated methodology should be available for integration of technology assessment and new product development. In industrial design engineering intensive research is ongoing with respect to methodology. Probably less work is carried out in the field of the methodology of technology assessment, but at least some work is being done.

Frost, for example, developed a model for technology assessment that employed a five-stage approach:

- Stage 1: Establish market place requirements;
- Stage 2: Identify Technology Solutions;
- Stage 3: Classify the technology solutions;

- Stage 4: Establish sources of technology acquisition;
- Stage 5: Finalize the technology acquisition decision;

For the technology acquisition decision, Frost defined eight criteria: time, cost, risk, organizational viability, strategy, organization learning, core competences and protection. It would be interesting to integrate the approach of Frost with the three aspects of "utility, functionality and usability" discussed in the foregoing. The Frost model does not extend to include the aspect of "usability". Solving usability problems in many cases calls for intensive technological developments. For example: The basic technology for navigation systems in cars was available many years before adequate solutions for the human interface problems were found, and this could be applied.

7.   Constraints with respect to the application of technology

It would probably even be defensible to postulate that today, usability problems are of greater importance than functionality and utility problems. This statement accords with the conclusions of Durrani (1999), who argues that there is often no shortage of technologies or creative ideas, but there are difficulties with the selection and incorporation of technologies into products. He attributes that to:

- Poor integration between technology acquisition and product development processes;
- Tenuous links between markets needs, product attributes and technology availability/demand.

Two basic kinds of technology could be defined:

- Technology which enables new functions (functionality technology);
- Technology, enabling the user to use this technology (usability technology).

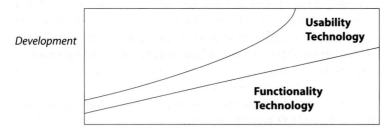

Development

Usability Technology

Functionality Technology

Figure 4
Functionality versus usability technology

As technological possibilities develop, the proportions of these two categories change in the direction of usability technology.

Durrani participated in the development of a tool, comprised of an information bank, a technology acquisition process and an information gallery. This tool, called MANTRA, made it possible to assess options on the basis of agreed criteria. In the past, much time and effort went into the development and exploitation of databases for technology transfer (Technotec, Dvorkovitch, etc.). However, these databases were hardly used by industrial designers. This can be explained by the earlier statement that, first and foremost, designers need leads. Databases cannot provide leads and are moreover only one of many different opportunities for follow-up.

8.   The architect as technology broker

Hargadon et al (1997). studied a large design agency in the US (IDEO) with respect to the function of designers as technology brokers. According to Hargadon, a technology broker "facilitates transactions between actors lacking access to, or trust in, one another". Brokers function in "disconnected networks". They can function as brokers thanks to the fact that they are well connected in several networks rather than extremely central in just one. With respect to the transfer process, Hargadon et al. distinguish five steps:

- Step 1. Access,
- Step 2. Acquisition,
- Step 3. Storage,
- Step 4. Retrieval,
- Step 5: Output.

IDEO has developed a methodology handbook for internal use. With respect to technology it says: "Working with companies in such dissimilar industries as medical instruments, furniture, toys and computers has given us a broad view of the latest technologies, materials and components available". The company compares itself with Edison's laboratory: "to bring together flows of information at the right moment". The goal of IDEO is to go "from serendipity to systematic access" of technical knowledge. It even calls itself a "clearinghouse for technological solutions". It is interesting to learn that it regards "organizational memory" as a thread as well as opportunity for innovation. It can hold the designer to existing solutions, but it can also bring solutions from one domain to another and new combinations of technologies.

The ideas of IDEO are completely absent in books on design methodology and management. Jones, for example, in his famous book "Design Methods", devotes only one page of attention to knowledge acquisition, namely in relation to literature searches. There is no attention for networking, links to research etc. It is striking that thoughts about technology transfer in the context of industrial product design are not found in the established handbooks on industrial design engineering. Of course, Bruce Archer mentions research in his models, but the transfer process itself is ignored.

9. Integration of research and design

Designers should become inspired by research and researchers should be inspired by design. Van den Kroonenberg (1992) claims that technology transfer is only possible when researchers and industrial designers each try to meet the other halfway. That is necessary because of the fact that they work from a complete different perspective.

Research activities result in new knowledge and design results in new artifacts. In research "analysis" prevails and in design "synthesis". The analysis leads to conclusions and the synthesis to decisions. In fact ,Van den Kroonenberg shows a black and white image of the phenomenon of research and design. Analysis and synthesis are elements, which are important in both design and in research. The data, used in the synthesis phase of the design process, should come from the analysis of the results of the information acquisition, which belongs to the design process. In research, synthesis is necessary to translate the results of analysis into hypothesis.

Research and design are not wholly unrelated fields. On the contrary: design includes an element of research, while research unmistakably has a design element.

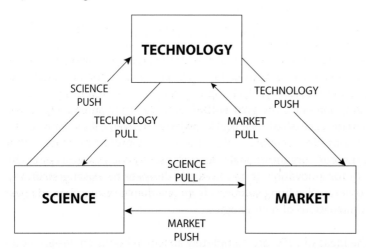

Figure 5
The science/market/technology triangle by Van den Kroonenberg (1992)

Another model of van den Kroonenberg shows the relationship between market, science and technology. Every combination shows a pull and a push effect as far as it concerns knowledge transfer. Van

[1] Also Eekels and Roozenburg (1991) studied the subject of the integration of research and design in "A methodological comparison of the structures of scientific research and engineering design: their similarities and differences" (Design Studies, vol. 12, no 4, October 1991, p197-203)

den Kroonenberg claims that the 'players' in each of the boxes need to be interested in the activities in the other boxes in order to make the transfer process work properly. Direct contact between market and science/technology is scarce. The industrial designer probably functions as a representative of the market. [1]

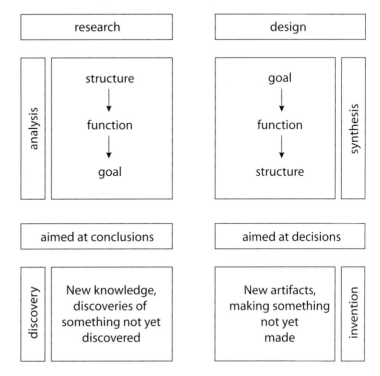

Figure 6
Differences between design and research, according to Van den Kroonenberg (1992)

10.   Conclusions

This paper should be regarded as an initiative to discuss the design of the façade of the future from a a design-methodological point of view. It would be interesting to see if innovation in the design process will lead us to innovation in façade design. There are many examples of products were a new paradigm was the starting point of a successful product range. Instead of starting the paper with a proposition I would this time like to end with a proposition:

Applying (for architecture) new insights, with respect to product innovation, to the design of facades will inevitably lead to new concepts for facades, which will meet the complex of interests of stakeholders.

References

Archer, L Bruce (1975). Design Awareness and Planned Creativity in Industry, Design Cncl, London, ISBN-10: 0850720168

Butter, E.F.M. (1989). Product Assessment: een Hulpmiddel bij het Formuleren en Beheersen van de Productstrategie, Kluwer, Deventer

Cooper, Robert G. (2001). Winning at New Products. 3rd edition, Addison-Wesley, Amsterdam.

Durrani, Tariq S. , Forbes Sheila M., Broadfoot, Charles & Carrie, A.S (1998), Managing the Technology Acquisition Process. Technovation, vol. 18, nrs. 8/9, p. 523-528.

Eekels J. (1982). Industriële Doelontwikkeling, Van Gorkum Assen.

Eekels, J. & Poelman, W.A. (1997). Trilogie Industriële Producton-twikkeling, deel 1 t/m 3. Lemma, Utrecht.

Eekels, J. & Roozenburg, N.F.M. (1991), "A methodological comparison of the structures of scientific research and engineering design: their similarities and differences". Design Studies, vol 12, no 4, p. 197-203.

Forbes, Naushad & Wield, D. (2000), "Managing R&D in technology-followers", Research Policy, vol. 29, nr. 9, p.1095-1109.

Frost, Richard B. (1992). "A converging model of the design process analysis and creativity, the ingredients of synthesis". Journal of Engineering Design, vol. 13, nr 2, p. 117-126.

Hargadon, Andrew & Sutton, Robert I. (1997). "Technology Brokering and Innovation in a Product Development Firm". Administrative Science Quarterly, vol. 42, December, p 716-749.

Hadi Teherani – Bothe Richter Teherani, Lecture at the University of Applied Science in Detmold, 06.Aug. 2007

Jones, John Chris. (1992), Design Methods, 2nd edition, Van Nostrand Reinhold, New York.

Kroonenberg, H.H. van den & Siers, F.J. (1992). "Methodisch Ontwerpen", Educaboek., Culemborg

Morita, Akio. (1986). Made in Japan: Akio Morita & Sony, E.P. Dutton/ Plume, New York.

Muller, W. (2001). Order and Meaning in Design, Lemma, Utrecht

Poelman W.A. (1990), Ontwerpers in de Industrie, Rathenau Institute, The Hague:

Poelman, W.A. (1996). De Rol van het CME bij de Introductie en Toepassing van Jessi, Centrum voor Micro-elektronica, Veenendaal.

Poelman W.A. (2004) Technology management in Product Design, Proceedings of the Lausanne Conference on Tools and Methods of Competitive Engineering, 2004 p. 73-81

Poelman W.A. (2002) Technology management in Product Design, Proceedings of the Wuhan Conference on Tools and Methods of Competitive Engineering, 2004 p.

Prakke, Frits & Varkevisser, Allan (ed.) (1996). Technologie in Politiek Perspectief , Hoofdstuk 8, Wetenschappelijk Bureau D' 66, 1996, 102-122.

Rakers, Georg, (1995), Introductiecursus Industrieel Ontwerpen, Poelman Partners, Zeist

Rogers, Everett M. (2003), Diffusion of Innovations, 5th edition. The Free Press, New York.

Roozenburg, N.F.M. & Eekels, J. (1995), Industrial Product Design: Fundamentals and Methods, Wiley , New York

The process of building facades encompasses many different parties, beginning with the user and ending with the supplier of buildings systems. The process therefore requires certain ways of decision making.

Prof. Dr. ir. Joop Hallman focuses on the building process from planning to final construction, and the possibilities of innovation within. How can a façade product ultimately meet the needs of the consumer?

The Future Envelope 1 – A Multidisciplinary Approach. U. Knaack and T. Klein (Eds.). IOS Press, 2008.

INDUSTRIAL BUILDING SYSTEMS DESIGN & ENGINEERING

Accelerating change through research and education

Joop Halman

Department of Construction
Management & Engineering
Faculty of Engineering
University of Twente

1.   Introduction

There is an overall concern in society that the building industry is underachieving. It has a relatively low profitability, and invests too little in capital, research and development and training. It also has a poor performance with regards to sustainability. The building industry and the built environment as a whole account for at least forty percent of energy consumption (EC, 2002). The construction sector also consumes about 40% of all extracted materials and accounts for high levels of non-renewable, non-recyclable materials and waste (Kibert, 2000). The building industry is further challenged by a yearly decrease in skilled construction workers. And last but certainly not least, too many of the building industry's clients are dissatisfied with its overall performance. Ambitions to improve this situation have led to reform initiatives in various countries in the past few years (see e.g. Flanagan et al., 2001; Egan, 2002; Ang et al., 2004). A wide range of improvements needed in the project process were identified, including the development of long-term relationships or partnering rather than competitive tendering, the development of Key Performance Indicators (KPIs) and greater standardization, together with improved leadership and customer focus. It set some challenging targets for on-time delivery, reduced costs, fewer defects, improved profitability, and health and safety (Macmillan, 2006). Although most of these initiatives have proven to be of value, one may characterize the achievements as relatively incremental. However, to tackle the identified challenges effectively, a more fundamental shift is needed in the building industry. The sustainability of this industrial sector is dependent on an essential change in the way resources are used, from non-renewables to renewables, from high levels of waste to high levels of reuse and recycling, and from products based on lowest first cost to those based on life-cycle costs and full costs accounting. The construction sector can seize the urgency to reform itself towards a sustainable sector to also transform its dominant business model. This means, to change from a primarily capacity driven building sector with a clear split between design and realization processes towards an entrepreneurial oriented sector that develops and realizes integrated and customized industrialized building solutions for target customers.

This paper will discuss some prerequisites that are necessary to realize this intended transformation process in the building industry. It will also elaborate on the implications for creating the future sustainable façade envelope. Research can accelerate this desired transformation process, by providing the necessary directions and insights for successful change. A new Master of Science program is proposed to educate professionals who are better qualified to meet the requirements that are asked for in the building industry of tomorrow. In contrast with the existing education programs in architecture, this new master program will provide students with the right mindset to develop innovative and sustainable building solutions that meet customer requirements.

2.   The voice of the customer

A principal shortcoming in most building companies is the almost complete absence of the marketing discipline. As a consequence, there is no clear vision and strategy about a company's target customers, their profile, their specific requirements and potential future needs. However, companies are being forced to respond to the growing individualization of demand. To produce this required variety at acceptable cost, it is important to know how customers prioritize the different design alternatives. However, there is still a lack of knowledge when it comes to the way in which building clients make choices and what customer priorities are in a mass customized environment (Dellaert and Stremersch, 2005). Therefore, building companies should initiate marketing research that focuses on investigating how potential building clients prioritize the different elements in a building design. This will help them in developing and selecting the right portfolio of options that meet the differentiated needs of target customers.

Hofman et al (2006), have conducted a vignette-based survey in the Netherlands among potential buyers of new houses. They investigated how potential buyers of new houses prioritize the different elements such as bathroom, kitchen and roof type of a house design. One main outcome of their study is the priority listing of housing attributes as shown in figure 1. This priority listing is of great importance for all building companies who offer or are considering offering customized housing. Building developers may deduct from this listing what potential buyers regard as being the most important housing attributes within customized solutions. This priority listing will help building developers in their decision making about the right balance between the variety (such as different types of bathrooms, kitchens and roof types) to be offered versus the need to standardize and produce at acceptable cost. Although people in general prefer to have the opportunity to select from options, they will be less interested if such options also mean an increased price. A second principal contribution of the study of Hofman et al (2006) has been the discovery of the trade¬ off relationships between customer value and the price of the distinguished dimensions of housing attributes. The difference between perceived customer value and price can be used as a measure of the incentive for the customer to buy. To outperform competitors, it is proposed that house builders follow a strategy of maximizing this difference. A limitation of the study of Hofman et al concerns the country specific nature of priorities.

One might question to what extent the results will also be applicable in other countries. Repeating this research outside The Netherlands would reveal to what extent potential buyers of new houses in other countries differ in prioritizing attributes in house design. The approach that Hofman et al followed could also be replicated for other segments in the building industry.

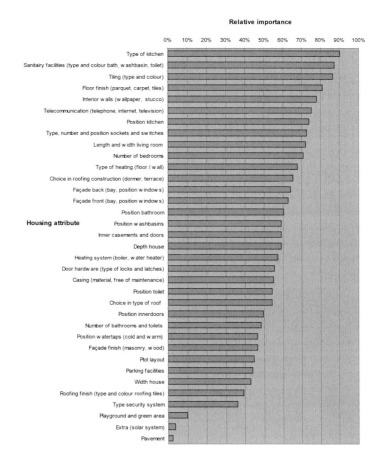

Figure 1
Housing attributes: Relative importance for potential buyers (Hofman et al, 2006)

3.   Product platforms and product family development

An important consequence of the need to offer a variety of options and elements from which customers can select the one that best meets their needs is that building companies will have to become capable of developing strategies for achieving optimum balances between standardization and variation. Customer-focused design strategies based on the creation of product families sharing common module-based platforms are receiving world wide interest. In industries as diverse as electronics, software, automobile and domestic appliances, module-based product platforms have already proved successful (Meyer and Lehnerd, 1997; Meyer et al, 1997; Salvador et al., 2002; Ulrich, 1995).

Until recently, no systematic methods were applied in the building industry for evaluating the applicability of modules and product platforms. However a new methodology for developing product platforms in the specific of the house building industry is now available (Veenstra et al, 2006). The applicability of this methodology has been tested at a Dutch house building company. In this study, the methodology demonstrated its added value in determining which modules to standardize and defining a product platform (see figure 2). Although only the house building industry has been the focus in this research, as is the case with the Hofman et al (2006) study, one might also consider extending the application of the methodology in comparable building industries such as the development and construction of offices and other utility buildings.

4.   Organizing the supply chain

If a building developing company decides to apply a modular-based product platform approach to create a variety of building solutions at acceptable costs, it will also need to decide which parts this company will develop and/or manufacture in-house and for which parts design and/or manufacturing will be outsourced to external parties. The type of supplier relationship not only depends on the internal availability of the required capabilities or resources of the company concerned, but also on the uniqueness of the module or component that a supplier might offer and on the re-use potential of the specific module or component in the product family.

Basically there are two types of supplier networks. In a centralised network, suppliers are tied to a lead firm. This lead firm demands large numbers of parts from its suppliers and as a consequence offers stability of sales for these supplying firms. The lead firm has the power to determine standards and interfaces between the different modules and components. Examples of these types of lead firms in the building industry are house manufacturers such as Sekisui, National House, Daiwa and Toyota Homes (Gann, 1996). None of these companies evolved from traditional craft house building, but were started by large conglomerates, which were able to invest heavily in factory facilities and R&D. All these type of building firms employ several hundred of scientists, technologists, ergonomists, architects and engineers. In a decentralized network, however, because of limitations in scale of demand, it is hard to function

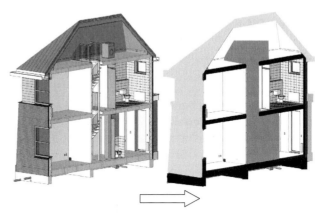

Module specification

| Core | Structure | Traffic Space |

| | **Extension modules** | **Built-in modules** |

Floor plan	Extension Living room	Bathroom
	Garage	Kitchen
	Storage	(Bed)room
	Bay window	
	Dormer	

Finishes

| Exterior (building style) | Interior |

Figure 2
Example of specification and hierarchy of modules (Veenstra et al, 2006)

as a lead firm and extremely difficult to impose industrial standards. Supplying firms will have to meet the needs of diverse clients and are often reluctant to adapt their production system to the specific needs of one specific client. As a consequence standards can only be determined through a negotiation process in which suppliers and assemblers jointly participate and recognize benefits to standardize specific elements such as interfaces between the different elements or modules in the building industry. A similar process has taken place in the past in the kitchen industry where developers of systems for kitchens mutually agreed on standard dimensions for kitchen cupboards, for dishwashers, microwaves etc. The result is that infinite competitive options for kitchen system designs can be created while using the standard dimensions agreed on. The building industry would greatly benefit if supplying and assembling parties also agree on setting certain standards e.g. on the use of specific interfaces between building elements, the use of ICT tools etc. It will depend on the emergence of business champions in this sector to what extent options to agree and settle for certain standards will be realized successfully.

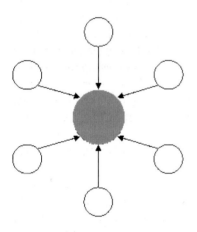 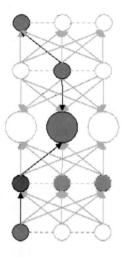

Figure 3
Centralized versus decentralized network (Langlois and Robertson, 1992)

5.   Sustainability and Innovation

In the introduction part of this paper we have stressed the need to drastically change the building industry into a sustainable building industry. Innovative solutions are called for to the way natural resources are used, both in the design and production phase of buildings as well as in their exploitation phase. So far, construction is usually classified as a traditional or low-technology sector with low levels of expenditure on activities associated with innovation, such as research and development (OECD, 2000; Seaden and Manseau, 2001). The main drivers of technological change in the building industry are seen to be new components introduced by suppliers to the industry. Reichstein et al (2005) however also discuss a series of case studies in which construction firms showed to be able to successfully make a range of different organizational, managerial or technological innovations to overcome the limits of their environment.

Besides suppliers and construction firms, also government can play a role in stimulating innovation. Government could improve technology commercialization by either stimulating the commercialization of various competing technologies or developing various competing products based on the same technology (Caerteling et al, 2008).

6. System integrators and system integration

The subject of interorganizational cooperation in relation to innovation has been receiving attention in two fields of literature (Rutten et al, 2007). Firstly, in construction management literature scholars have argued that it is interorganizational cooperation across project boundaries in particular, that is important for innovation in construction industry (Dewick & Miozzo, 2004; Doreé & Holmen, 2004; Holmen et al., 2005; Miozzo & Dewick, 2004). Close and stable relations between the various organizations involved in the construction process, such as contractors, architects, engineers, suppliers, clients, research institutes and government bodies, appears to contribute to the development and adoption of innovations. It is also argued that close and stable relations facilitate sharing of knowledge and risks. Secondly, in literature on complex product systems industries, scholars focus on the role of systems integrators in the innovation process. Systems integrators perform a leadership role in interorganizational cooperation. They add value through systems integration: they integrate components, technologies, skills and knowledge from various organizations into a unified product or product family that meets specific customer needs. To do so, systems integrators set up a strategic network of organizations and coordinate the process of integrating dispersed resources of the network members. Notwithstanding its recognized importance in the innovation process, the role of systems integrators is still an underresearched topic in the innovation management literature and needs further exploration.

7. New models for business development in the building industry

Recent developments such as new systems of procurement and integrated contracts require a change in the still dominant capacity driven business model of the building industry. To stay competitive, companies will need to change their mind set towards a business development orientated approach. This means a definite farewell of the one-of-a kind type of projects, specifically designed and realized on the request of a singular client towards the creation of a family of differentiated building solutions to meet the specific needs of target customers. In the coming years different business models will probably emerge in the building industry. Design oriented research can be of help to investigate what are the successful business models to apply given specific contexts in the building sector.

8. Towards a new Master in Industrial Building systems Design and Engineering

The building sector is changing its scope from 'design from scratch' towards mass customization. As a result, modules and subsystems are more frequently prefabricated in factories instead of constructed on-site (see figure 4). However, current master programs in architecture still focus on the design of one-of-a-kind objects. Student architects also too often erroneously develop the idea that they will later play a "Prima Donna" role in the building process. Students who follow a master program in Industrial Design often develop the right industrial mind set but lack the context knowledge about building processes and also the content knowledge about subjects such as building materials and building physics. There is a need for a different type of Master of Science program to educate professionals that are better qualified to meet the requirements that are asked for in the building industry of tomorrow. These master students will be able to design building components and systems from an industrial design and production perspective while also taking into account cost and human aspects and customer needs among which aesthetics and ease of use.

Industrial Building systems Design and Engineering (IBDE) concerns the development of new building components or new building systems (a set of interrelated components) and adds to the existing master programs of Industrial Design that primarily focus on the development of professional and consumer products. Building components are mostly business-to-business products. However, buildings or structures as a whole can sometimes also be regarded as consumer products. Furthermore, buildings are not just products to be used but also objects for investments. Long life times exceeding 40 years and large sizes of products for the building sector, ask for a different approach than applied yet to common consumer products. For instance, aspects such as costs, long term quality, customization, adaptability, platforms, manufacturing and environmental sustainability will play another role in the product development process.

Finally, in the industrial building sector, the product development process is mostly a multi-disciplinary and multi-stakeholder process in which a single client cannot be determined easily. To meet the new requirements for professionals who will act in a building sector in transformation, students need to get experience study and work on the following main topics:

- Building systems design solutions (aesthetics, ease of use, system integration)
- Sustainable solutions (energy and building materials related subjects)
- Manufacturing design (how to realize the developed systems at acceptable costs)
- Building process design (how to organize and manage the building process effectively and efficiently)
- Industrial marketing (taking customer perspective as design drive) and Cost management

Figure 4
Examples of fabrication of modules and subsystems (NCC and Burggraaf)

9. Future professionals in façade development

Education can accelerate the required changes that are called for in the building sector. With respect to the future envelope, the topic of the symposium at the Faculty of Architecture, the proposed master program may e.g. include final assignments that challenge students to create new types of facades that meet the new requirements of sustainability, that are appealing from an aesthetical point of view but that can also be produced in an industrial setting. Two examples of final assignments in façade development that one might think of are:

1. Investigate the options to integrate climate systems in Glass facades
   Type of firm: Supplier of Glass facades
   Research and design activities to be performed are:
   - Analysis of climate systems
   - Analysis of facades
   - Analysis of integration options
   - System design and evaluation of alternatives
   End result: High tech new facade

2. Develop an integrated roof system based on advanced solar technology
   Type of firm: Supplier of roof systems
      • Analysis of solar technology systems
      • Analysis of roof systems
      • Develop an integrated system based on case study design
      • Evaluate pro's and con's
      • Develop product platform and product range
   End result: Design of a "power roof".

10. Conclusion

To meet the challenges of sustainability and innovation, a fundamental shift is required in the building industry. To stay competitive, building firms will have to adopt new entrepreneurial business models. Customizing building concepts, stable partnerships, systems integration, the creation of product platforms and product families are some of the ingredients that will characterize these new business models. To accelerate the process towards a sustainable and innovative building sector students with a different profile in education are required.

References

Caerteling, J.S., Halman, J.I.M. and Dorée, A.G. (2008) Technology Commercialization in road infrastructure: how government affects the variation and appropiability of technology, Journal of Product Innovation Management, special issue on technology commercialization (forthcoming).

Dellaert , B.G.C. and Stremersch, S. (2005) Marketing mass-customized products: striking a balance between utility and complexity, Journal of Marketing Research, 42: 219-227.

Dewick, P., and Miozzo, M. (2004). Networks and innovation: Sustainable technologies in scottish social housing. R & D Management, 34(3): 323-333.

Doreé, A. G., & Holmen, E. (2004). Achieving the unlikely: Innovating in the loosely coupled construction system. Construction Management and Economics, 22(8): 827-838.

Egan, J. (2002) Accelerating change, a report by the strategic management forum for construction chaired by Sir John Egan, Construction Industry Council, London.

European council (EC) 2002 Energy performance building directive (EPBD), Directive 2002/91/EC of the European parliament and of the council of 16 december 2002 on the energy performance of buildings.

Gann, D.M. (1996) Construction as a manufacturing process? Similarities and differences between industrialized housing and car production in Japan, Construction Management and Economics 14: 437-450.

Hofman, E., Halman, J.I.M. and Ion, R.A. (2006) variation in housing design: identifying customer preferences, Housing Studies, 21(6): 929-943.

Holmen, E., Pedersen, A. C., & Torvatn, T. (2005). Building relationships for technological innovation. Journal Of Business Research, 58(9): 1240-1250.

Kibert, C.J., Sendzimir, J. and Guy, B., Construction ecology and metabolism: natural system analogues for a sustainable built environment, Construction management and Economics, 18: 903-916.

Langlois, R.N. and Robertson, P.L. (1992) Networks and innovation in a modular system: lessons from the microcomputer and stereo component industries, Research Policy, 21: 297-313.

Macmillan, S. (2006) Chronicles of the revolution, Building Research & Information, 34(6): 600-603.

Meyer, M.H., Lehnerd, A.P. (1997) The power of product platforms: building value and cost leadership, Free press, NY.

Meyer, M.H. Tertzakian, P. and Utterback, J.M. (1997) Metrics for measuring research and development in the context of the product family, Management Science 43(1):88-111.

Miozzo, M., & Dewick, P. (2004). Networks and innovation in european construction: Benefits from inter-organisational cooperation in a fragmented industry. International Journal Of Technology Management, 27(1): 68-92.

OECD (2000) Technology policy: an international comparison of innovation in major capital projects, Organization for Economic Co-operation and Development, Paris.

Rutten, M.E.J., Dorée, A.G. and Halman, J.I.M. (2007) Interorganizational cooperation in innovation: the role of systems integrators, Proceedings of the ManuBuild 1st International Conference, The transformation of the Industry: Open Building manufacturing, 25-26 April 2007, Rotterdam, The Netherlands.

Seaden, G. and Manseau, A. (2001) Public Policy and Construction Innovation, Building Research and Information, 29(3): 603-612.

Salvador F, Forza C, Rungtusanatham M (2002) Modularity, product variety, production volume, and component sourcing: theorizing beyond generic prescriptions. Journal of Operations Management, 20 (5): 549-575

Ulrich, K. (1995) The role of product architecture in the manufacturing firm, Research Policy 24(3): 419-440.

Veenstra, V.S., Halman, J.I.M. and Halman, J.I.M. (2006) A methodology for developing product platforms in the specific setting of the house building industry, Research in Engineering Design, 17: 157-173.

How can we think about façade design and development without thinking about architecture? The goal of **Ir. Michiel Cohen**, as principal of Cepezed, is to create efficient and lightweight buildings. According to his philosophy, it is essential to know and control the entire building process in order to create customized facades with the necessary respect for industry and standardization.

The Future Envelope 1 – A Multidisciplinary Approach. U. Knaack and T. Klein (Eds.). IOS Press, 2008.

THE FUTURE ENVELOPE

Towards a More Reactive Facade

Michiel Cohen, Joost Heijnis

Cepezed Architects

It may be a terrible message for our profession. Unknowingly to most people facades have always defined our environment. And facades have been mainly been defined by other factors than architecture. Architects however maintain the opposite. They believe they are creating the facades. The contrary however is all around us.

Some years ago a colleague asked after a lecture about cepezed architecture whether it would be possible to imagine a city made of steel and glass. It was answered by returning the question: "Could mediaeval man imagine a city of brick?" Time and other factors define the answer, not the material.

To understand the future of the envelope it is essential to understand its past. Where it came from, where it stands. Facades are in principle very simple means of creating shelter. Identical to roofs, but the roof has miraculously resisted all specialists and retained its simplicity. And facades have gone wild and unintelligibly complicated. Why?

Figure 1
"Could medieval man imagine a city of brick?"

Basic shelter started with cover against rain and wind. This gradually evolved in more advanced shelters which provided insulation to prevent loss of heat and in hot climates a cool environment. When mankind became more conscious about energy loss and cared more about comfort things were getting out of hand:

Figure 2
Basic shelter without added (complicated) requirements.

When walls became thicker- in stone due to fire protection - , the thermal capacity of the building increased: this caused thermally slow reacting buildings which, once cooled down, require a lot of energy to heat up. To accomplish this re-heating capacity, costly installations are introduced. Another problem is that the effect on the inside temperature due to outside temperature oscillations is shifted: high mass requires a long reaction time which might be comfortable but in most cases leads to even more technical installations.

Effect of thermal mass on inside temperatures

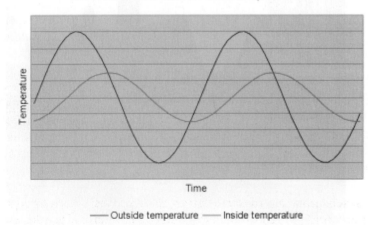

Figure 3
The effect of outside temperature oscillations on inside temperature.

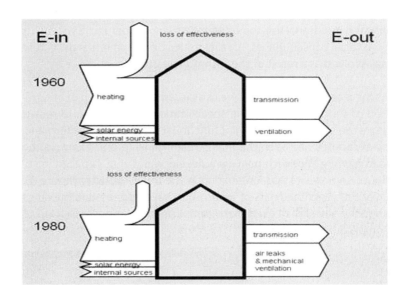

Figure 4
Transition in energy loss: from transmission to ventilation [2]

Next came high insulation values and maximized air tightness. This consequently gave ventilation and condensation problems. Mechanical ventilation devices were called in. These are costly and difficult to tune. These installations have become responsible for high energy use and loss (figure 4) and thereby working contrarily.

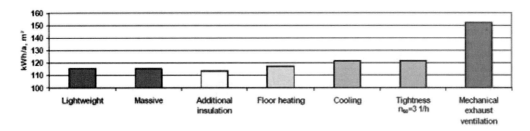

Figure 5
The effect of several different properties of a building on the energy demand [1].

In general it can be said that problems of the façade to be solved introduced other (much larger) problems. Besides that, the solutions also had more and more effect on the building itself and therefore shifted complications from the already complicated façade system to the rest of the building.

It is clear that whenever any further requirement is added to the primordial façade, problems arise. Temperature, humidity, light, acoustics, fire, smoke exhaust, ventilation, energy use, have progressively muddled our thinking on facades, complicating them unknowingly more than needed. Consequently the façade has become one of the most costly parts of a building.

Façade technology runs from leaves, skins, textiles, timber, through stone, brick, and concrete to glass, steel, aluminum and plastics. Every step in material use comes with its own cost-benefit, and with its own social consequences. Parallel to this development architecture has evolved as a result of the technical possibilities and needs.

As for recent developments we can discern the definition of integration of functions against the specialization of functions. In recent years the idea of integration of functional services and performances of facades has been the mainstream thinking. For example the load bearing sandwich panel is a development that cepezed introduced some years ago, originating in the trailer industry (figure 6). Over the years the limits of integration have appeared in buildings and they have led to even more complicated solutions which led to complicated solutions

Figure 6
The sandwichpanel evolved into a building component which led to complicated solutions

Therefore solutions should be simpler, more basic and compact. The façade should be the climate regulating skin it once was. Reacting dynamically without aesthetical consequences. Such solutions could be found in intelligent surface technology, membranes and even nanotechnology.

Cepezed has been using membranes in buildings for over a decade. The purpose of these membranes (perforated steel as well as open woven PTFE coated glass fiber, see figures 7 and 8) ranges from windbreaker, fence, radiation screen to sunscreen and often a combination of such functions.

The urban planning and architectural design methods are very traditional. Demands on every level of planning have evolved greatly. Neither in the functioning of buildings, nor in that of cities rigidity is

Figure 7
The use of textiles in façade technology: Westraven office building Utrecht

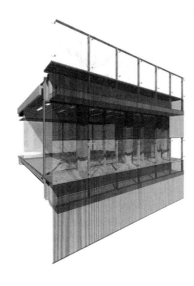

Figure 8
Perforated steel screens used in the design of the Centre for Human Drug Research, CHDR (1995) in Leiden, the Netherlands (by cepezed)

of any durable value anymore. So the teleological thinking in the design methods and results is outdated. Any plan should be a step in a continuous process of development. This has been called earlier 'pliable planning' [3].

Since the façade defines the potential of a building more than any other element, the façade should become pliable as well. Pliability could be achieved in many ways. In a technical field by moveable parts or by interchangeable parts. The first is the usual opening window or hatch, the last a system of replaceable and interchangeable elements.

That was the way it was. The future will be materials that can perform the same way.

Cepezed dares to invite the industry to pick up this challenge and join us for better building technology.

The new elements we are introducing today are aerodynamics, fil-

Figure 5
Nanotubes: ventilation valves of the future?

tering and flexibility. The goals are membranes, nanotechnology and molecular development to achieve this.

Pliable insulation values, transparency, airtightness, pliable water-tightness and vapour permeability must be developed for the future envelope.

The technology exists to create new architecture, and a new and a even more durable built environment.

The future should be more simple.

References

[1]   Jokisalo ,J and Kurnitski, J Effect of the thermal inertia and other building and HVAC factors on energy performance and thermal comfort in Finnish apartment buildings, REPORT B7, Teknillinen korkeakoulu. Konetekniikan osasto. LVI-tekniikan laboratorio. B Helsinki University of Technology. Department of Mechanical Engineering. Laboratory of Heating, Ventilating and Air Conditioning. B Espoo 2005, Finnland

[2]   Cohen, M.E., Lecture, Durabilité dans le bâtiment selon le concept de cepezed, Arene Ile-de-France, Concours l'Esquisse verte 4ème édition , 5ème Conférence Lundi 19 mars 2007, Paris

[3]   Cohen, M.E., Article, Pooibaar plannen, Beter bouwen en bewonen edition 26 part 4, STT/Beweton, Den Haag 2004

The work of **Prof. Dipl.-Ing. Axel Thallemer** consistently crosses the borders between traditional disciplines – one reason why he was invited to contribute to this "Multidisplinary Approach". In 1994 he was founder and head of Festo Corporate Design and created, amongst other beautiful products, "Airtecture" - pneumatic lightweight constructions that made him well known amongst architects. His works are inspired by nature and are, in many cases, strongly related to architecture. Since 2004, Prof. Axel Thallemer is Dean of Industrial Design at Kunstuniversität Linz, Austria.

AFTERTHOUGHTS TO THE SYMPOSIUM

Axel Thallemer

Professor Technical Design
Academy of Fine Arts,
Hamburg. Dean of Industrial
Design Linz, Austria
Self-employed under Airena®

Examples from nature are used metododologically as catalysts for brainstorming. However, these examples are not merely copied, but rather serve to expand the scope of theoretical design ideas and the morphologic box of practical solutions.

It is interesting to see in how far the future development of building envelops will be geared toward limp membranes. As a general observation the current focus of building development moves more and more toward highlighting energetic and material related efficiency potentials.

Thereby, aspects of light construction naturally take center stage. If architecture would increasingly embrace the idea that nature can be used as a source of inspiration to develop ideas, a large morphologic box would be available to create completely new approaches by modular use of individual elements.

In addition to the realization of an envelope appropriate for the materials and functions in question, it is essential to think ahead while keeping in mind to minimize energy consumption, from the construction across the entire utilization period to the deconstruction and recycled use of the materials. Another increasingly important factor is the amount of complexity and the number of functions that can be integrated into a building component. Current technical solutions predominantly entail that a single material or a single building component comprises a single function. Future developments could, in analogy to nature, provide multi-functional integrated components. In how far the perfect material and energy related circular flow of nature can be reproduced remains to be seen.

The structural principles of exoskeleton and endoskeleton are far from being sufficiently employed within the building development of human artifacts. Traditionally, the building trade evolved between the poles of discovered caves and from wooden posts, found in nature, arranged in mobile frameworks, filled in with filling materials; be they of plant or animal origin. Thus, antipodal the natural composite from cellulose and lignin – in form of wood – plaid an important role besides the building material stone. Until today, the vast majority of material applications in the building industry derive from these origins. From natural stone to artificial stone to fiber-reinforced concrete materials on one hand, and from load-bearing beams, such as the tree grew in nature, to bent plywood plane load-bearing structures on the other. Metals were added as building materials when mankind learned to use fire and ore for specific purposes, followed by ceramic materials, and then glass. In early times, skins of animal or plant origin probably served as filling materials, later decollated into strong fibers and then reassembled into two-dimensional semi-finished parts.

Only since recently, new weaving methods make three-dimensional textiles seem possible. Today, progress in procedures and technologies in chemistry has made it possible to produce membranes as foils without fiber-bound carrier materials. Here, the surface is of special interest, because numerous characteristics can be influenced by coatings that could not be realized until recently. However, because the traditional building materials were used as basis for corresponding directives and regulations, it is accordingly difficult to adjust specific laws when new and different building components come into play. Without the adaptation of current building codes to new materials and their characteristics, it will not be possible to create sustainable innovations in the building industry.

Mathematical modeling and computer simulation allow us much more accurate prognoses in terms of a building component's behavior than was possible in the past. Before, experience as well as trial and error plaid a more important role than today, where we can draw on current technological possibilities.

In addition to new materials, manufacturing and assembly procedures as well as optimized calculation methods, interdisciplinary networking of individual contract subsections will become increasingly important in the future. Thus, continuous integration of sensor technology into individual building components is as predetermined as increasing the dynamics of building structures compared to the prevailing static building of our times.

Building structures that are self-regulating or even self-organizing and automatically adapt to the specific conditions are conceivable today, and they need not necessarily consist of traditional building materials but rather of fluidly pre-stressed limp membranes. These theoretical approaches can lead to entirely new solutions with regards to spaces for human occupation, be they on the earth, the moon or Mars. But these thoughts can also be employed for areas such as the aerospace industry as well as personal mobility.

The increasing fragmentation of specialized knowledge in the building industry can only be re-consolidated by cross-communication of various disciples. The dissolution of disciple-specific delimitation will be a key issue for the development of future building structures. It will be interesting to see which position architecture will adopt within the development process. Will formal aesthetics be the only thing to remain?

As a specialist in façade design and the execution of special constructions, **Prof. Dr. ir. Mick Eekhout** took on the role of head of research of the department Building Technology within the Faculty of Architecture / TU Delft. Research as one of the driving forces in façade innovation is placed in an overall larger picture. He describes his efforts to combine forces within and between the department, faculty, university and national institutions: a necessity when trying to establish a strong and fruitful research environment.

FUTURE FOR FAÇADE RESEARCH AT TU DELFT

Mick Eekhout

Professor of Product
Development
Nestor of Building Technology
Faculty of Architecture
Delft University of Technology

A warrior of light knows that he has much to be grateful for.

He was helped in his struggle by the angels; celestial forces placed each thing in its place, thus allowing him to give of his best.

His companions say: ' He's so lucky!' And the warrior does sometimes achieve things far beyond his capabilities.

That is why, at sunset, he kneels and gives thanks for the protective Cloak surrounding him.

His gratitude however, is not limited to the spiritual world; he never forgets his friends, for their blood mingled with his on the battlefield.

A warrior does not need to be reminded of the help given him by others; he is the first to remember and he makes sure to share with them any rewards he receives.

Paulo Coelho: Manual of the Warrior of Light;

1.   Introduction

Facades have been a part of research on the faculty of Architecture since 15 years. Prof. Jan Brouwer started research in the 1990s as 'the intelligent façade', a technical and architectural composition. In 1992 prof.Mick Eekhout started his quest for 'Zappi' the unbreakable structural transparent plate material. Many 2x2m² large façade prototypes were made by 3rd and 4th year students in the Laboratory of Product Development during the last 12 years as a part of the educational program of Building Technology. In 1997 Just Renckens received his PhD on his dissertation 'Façades and Architecture', an overview on the state of the art and a closer focus on double facades. [1] During the following ten years Renckens managed to organize a yearly TU Delft symposium on a façade related subject. At his goodbye symposium on 20 September 2005 the announcement was made that the topic of Façades would be taken over by the then newly appointed Prof. Dr. Ulrich Knaack at the Chair of

Design of Constructions.

In the new research portfolio of the department of Building Technology the research topic of Façades was introduced by Prof. Dr. Knaack as a firm program comprising not less than 5 PhD students, financed by the university thanks to a beneficial stream of stimulating grants, to be matched in due time by 3rd money financing. Prof. Dr. Knaack aspires to bring new impulses in the façade industry. He combines his professorial employments at the two universities of Delft and Detmold (Germany) to form an international façade master education.

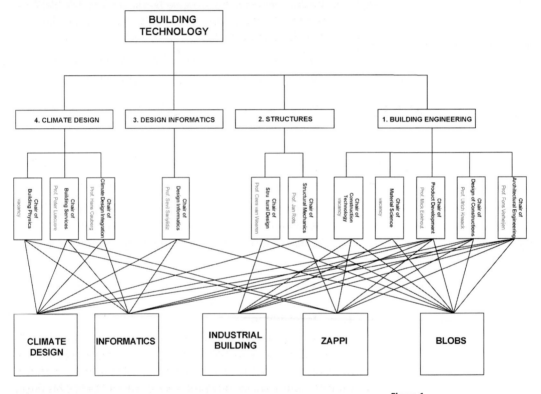

In the meantime the EU COST 13 commission 'Glass & Interactive Building Envelopes' was working on an international level between 2001 and 2006. The results of this commission were published in 2006 [2]. One of the main conclusions of Cost Action 13 is that "the three worlds of Architecture, Building Physics and Structural Engineering are today by far not sufficiently integrated"].

Figure 1
Relationships between 11 chairs and 5 research programs

The façade industry has grown more mature in the last 3 decades. What could university research contribute to that end? Product development of ingredients and new systems is an activity that each engineering department of a larger façade manufacturer should be able to accomplish. Most of the Dutch façade manufacturers depend on their system suppliers, like Schüco, Hueck and Reynolds, who continuously work on system improvements. Only a small number of the larger façade manufacturers are project-directed and able to make proposals for each new project. Their façade systems are project-systems. What academic research would be most beneficial for the Dutch façade industry? The Façades research team had to make a choice between perfecting the usual in ever refined details and automation of production and handling machine-operated windows? Or starting the quest for a revolutionary new approach? An approach that, like COST 13 indicated, links Architecture, Structural Engineering, Construction Design with Building Physics, Climate Design and Building Services. An integrated approach of Architecture, Construction and Climate Design: the integrated façade. The integrated façade is the chosen direction: a new generation of façades with an integrated materials + physics approach.

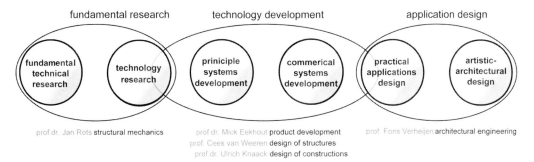

Figure 2
Six rings from fundamental research to free architectural design with 3 characteristic domains of Research, Development and Design.

2.   Current Research Portfolio And Facades

How does this Façade research group fit in the overall research plan? In the 'Meerjarenplan' of the department of Building Technology at TU Delft the following profile is given for the research of the department: The department focuses her scientific research on the domain of the Technology of Building. [3] This research has strong design relations, but stretches between the extreme ends of fundamental technical research and application directed design and includes technology development as her central domain. New knowledge and insight from this research is published in articles, books, conferences and symposiums and realised prototypes. More specifically the mission statement of the research points at the newness that has to be reached: "The department of Building Technology wants to precede the international practice with new knowledge and insight of building technology, both in theory, in designs, as well as in executed prototypes as in one-offs in the building practice. The results of this design research are used in teaching (research driven education)". The mission lies in developing science-based but inventive and innovative technical answers to new challenges at the interface between architectural and engineering design of buildings.

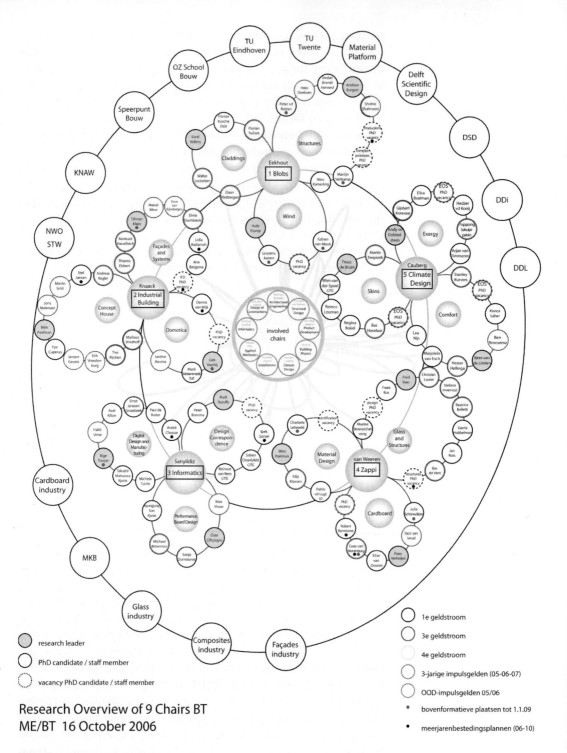

Research Overview of 9 Chairs BT
ME/BT 16 October 2006

Figure 3
Relations of 5 programs in Building
Technology Research, 15 subpro-
grams and some 80 researchers.

Major challenges include:
- Development of free-form computer-assisted technology ('Blobs'),
- Inventive use of new materials, techniques and systems ('Zappi'),
- Innovative developments for 'Concept House', 'Façades' and 'Domotica' ('Industrial Building')
- Smart Information Technology ('Informatics')
- Development of healthy, environmentally intelligent climates for sustainable buildings ('Climate Design').

All chairs of Building Technology collaborate cross linked in 5 integrated research programs, which are interesting to mention as all of these link to the façades program:

1. Blobs Structures, Claddings, Wind:
   15 to 20 researchers
   Research leader prof. Mick Eekhout
2. Industrial Building Concept House, Façades and Systems, Domotica:
   15 to 20 researchers
   Research leader prof. Ulrich Knaack
3. Informatics Digital Design and Manufacturing, Performance Based Design, Design Correspondence: 15 to 20 researchers
   Research leader prof. Sevil Sariyildiz
4. Zappi Glass and Structures, Material Design, Cardboard:
   15 to 20 researchers
   Research leader prof. Cees van Weeren
5. Climate Design Skins, Comfort, Exergy:
   15 to 20 researchers
   Research leader prof. Hans Cauberg

The scientific newness of this visually complicated set-up is in the design integration. The relevance of Building Technology lies in its combination of designs (creative, explorative, product-developing, combinatory) with technical and scientific depth (the disciplines in the 11 chairs). Research, Development and Designing are three main anchors in the research program of Building Technology. This couples impact in terms of striking new application designs with technology development and fundamental research, see figure 2. Today, ICT technology is complementing the state-of-affairs of conventional building and, more interesting in academic sense, pushing the frontiers of designing in complexity, for example designing of free-form building. Similarly, mechanics and materials science will boost innovations in designing with materials (glass, cardboard, glass fibre reinforced polyester, carbon fiber reinforced epoxy) construction and preservation techniques, while building physics and climate design will generate new concepts for indoor climate of buildings. In all programs, the scientific rules of theorizing, designing, modeling, testing, validating and prototyping will be followed, enriched with integrative design strategies towards practical applications.

Scientific research & development is requested to open towards society more than ever before. To an increasing extent, society calls for technology for individual 'free form' buildings, for the application of innovative materials and hybrids, (for techniques for the conservation and transformation of buildings and architectural heritage), and for buildings that are healthy, sustainable, and environmentally intelligent. Buildings are essential to our quality of life. People live, care, work, study, shop and relax in buildings. The integrated technology chain to design, engineer and produce buildings is consequently relevant to society. Building technology also contributes to a competitive and innovative residential and non-residential building industry.

Building Technology at TU Delft has gradually expanded its research portfolio and invited an (departmental / internal) peer review board in 5 colloquia for the 5 programs and an (university / external) Mid Term Review Board to advise on the quality of the research and the future of the 5 research programs of the department. The Façades subprogram of the program Industrial Building was a part of both reviews which took place in the form of the Industrial Buildings Colloquium on 8 February [4] and the Mid Term Review on 7 May 2007 [5] respectively.

These colloquia were organized in order to have all researchers distinctly define their own research for themselves and their supervisors, to acquaint all researchers with each others work, to give the opportunity for at least 3 external peers in each program to absorb the information and to speak out and write their peer advices to the department. The self study information was collected in 5 Colloquium Books, which contained a poster and an A4 format description of each project. These books also contained the more detailed presentations for a number of PhD students for their yearly 'VCW' Review. In order to complete the view on the research arena each Colloquium Book contained a number of scientific articles, at least one for each subprogram to illustrate the level of know how, insight and technology gained by research. These 5 books have been joined into this one Building Technology Projects Book, which was handed to the Mid Term Review Board and associated research professionals for their advice. During the last 4 years the number of PhD students quadrupled in the department of Building Technology and at the moment there are some 80 researchers in the department as a whole, amongst whom 50 PhD students and 30 staff and external PhD students. In the enthusiastic exploration of new research initiatives we send our PhD students on world wide conferences and they return after discussions with prominent peers in their fields of expertise, enriching the list of international contacts. The influence of internationalization is seen in the growing average quality of the research output.

3. Status Of The Subprogram Facades

In the midst of the 5 Building Technology programs the subprogram of Façades is initiated form the Chairs of Design of Constructions a (Prof. Knaack) and the Chair of Product Development (Prof. Eekhout). One of the statements after the peer reviews was that a large gain is to be obtained by integrating the subprogram Facades with the two subprograms Skins and Comfort, which are set up from the building physical basis. When facades are to be integrated into free form design buildings collaboration could be sought with the subprogram of Blobs / Claddings. In case progress is to be made on the pure material field, the Zappi program could be linked. In case of automation of movable parts in building, the program of informatics is to be linked up. This is the reason why in this article all 5 programs are illustrated.

4. Sixteen Steps Strategy

The Projects Book [5] displays the (standardized) results of the research organization of the department of Building Technology per 31 December 2006. It is a part of a longer term strategy which is displayed in figure 4, the so called "Sixteen Steps Strategy". This plan started with the extension of the research directly after the Qanu Research assessment in 2003, which was quite positive for the two programs 'Blobs/ICT' and 'Zappi' but less for the program Environments'. However, in this case the consequences of the positive assessment overwhelmed and the research portfolio was innovated, split up, expanded and exploded by the fortunate effects of a number of financial impulses from the faculty to get the research enriched. Some of these impulses were interpreted as to contain mandatory collaborations with the industry, so as to cover the remainder of 50% fees for the PhD students in question. Thus the effects of financial impulses were doubled. A step up into future independency through validation. The Sixteen Steps Strategy represents the growth into maturity of the research plan of Building Technology as a whole from the validation (step 3) via the peer reviews (step 8) and the Mid Term Review (step 11) to the tenders of large scale international research programs, which only will only be successful when the research group is independent, has enough critical mass and has a sufficiently scientific assessment.

Step 1: Growth
The total research staff and PhD students of Building Technology ex-

ploded between 1 January 2003 and 31 December 2006 (assessment period for the Mid Term) out of the stronger spirit in research, accelerated by the direct funding and impulses in funding in the faculty and of 3rd party funding.

Step 2: Arrangement

In 2006 the clustering of affiliated research projects was undertaken by the Research Nestor. The arrangement took place in 6 consequent steps, first to groups, in a smaller section of 3 Chairs and later of the total department, ending in the well-organized 'Satellite Scheme' of 15 sub-programs and 5 programs

Step 3: Validation

The proper qualitative data are collected: the output results in Delft BTA points is drafted by the secretariat. The rearrangement of the research in the satellite scheme by the Research Nestor is also a quantitative containment. The supervising professors are still fully responsible for the quality of the research under their supervision. The Peer Reviews produced a qualitative review, discussed by the complete group of program leaders and sub-program leaders. The result of the

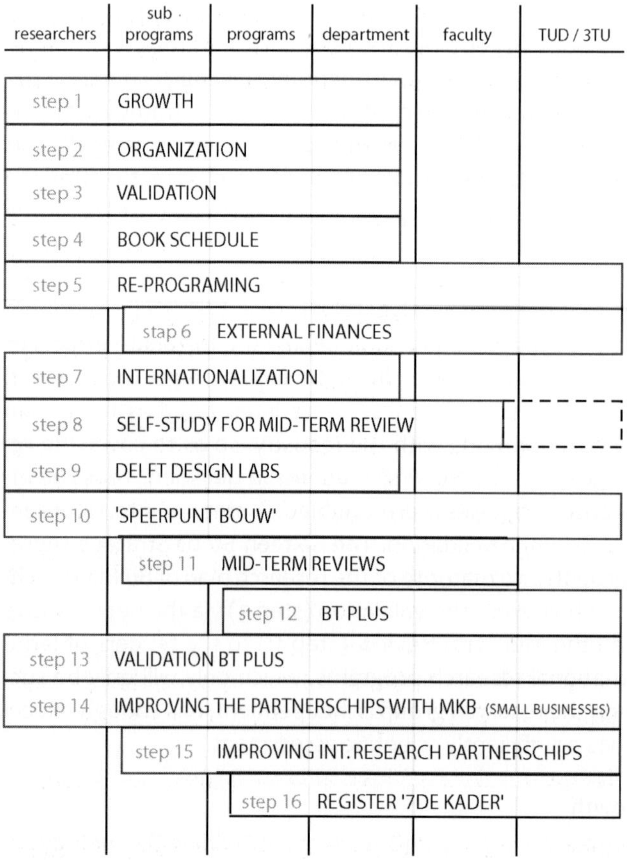

researchers	sub·programs	programs	department	faculty	TUD / 3TU
step 1	GROWTH				
step 2	ORGANIZATION				
step 3	VALIDATION				
step 4	BOOK SCHEDULE				
step 5	RE-PROGRAMING				
	stap 6	EXTERNAL FINANCES			
step 7	INTERNATIONALIZATION				
step 8	SELF-STUDY FOR MID-TERM REVIEW				
step 9	DELFT DESIGN LABS				
step 10	'SPEERPUNT BOUW'				
	step 11	MID-TERM REVIEWS			
		step 12	BT PLUS		
step 13	VALIDATION BT PLUS				
step 14	IMPROVING THE PARTNERSCHIPS WITH MKB (SMALL BUSINESSES)				
	step 15	IMPROVING INT. RESEARCH PARTNERSCHIPS			
		step 16	REGISTER '7DE KADER'		

Figure 4
Relationship 16 Steps, a consolidated 3TU Netherlands research approach.

peer reviews are specific actions as to the continuation or stopping of the research projects, advised by the peers but executed by the professors.

Step 4: Publication Plan

Depending of the newness and quality of the research topics a list of publications in international scientific magazines, in professional magazines (for valorization) and in monographs and books will be drafted to confirm the scientific content and societal impulses in lieu of the many conference papers given internationally.

Step 5: Towards Reprogramming

A number of causes will lead to a set-up of a new programming: the current programming was started in 2002 for a period of 6 years. Influences from the Delft Research Centre for Materials, the Delft Design Laboratories, the future Delft Research Centre 'Integrated Cities, Buildings & Components' and the 3TU collaboration and other initiatives. They all will lead to a reformatting of the programming.

Step 6: External Finances

In future the 1st money stream will probably be reduced and will have to be substituted by 3rd money and 2nd money. Third money experiences since 2,5 years in the Prometheus formula show that consortia of 4 industrial firms around one PhD student is achievable, but very labour-intensive to maintain.

Step 7: Internationalization

The international contacts of our researchers to chairs and research persons of different faculties lead to a diverse international network, which is used for exchange of lectures and workshops, occasional staff exchange, students per (semi-)semester, peer reviews from both sides and collaboration in supervision of common PhD researchers and common staff research projects.

Step 8: Peer Reviews for the Mid Term Review

The preparations for the Mid Term Review contain self studies, internal debates and the highly technical specialized Peer Reviews on the presented body of research. The Building Technology Projects Book is the result.

Step 9: Delft Design Labs participation

These collaborations have started in February 2007 and will be expanded in future and influence the future reprogramming.

Step 10: Delft Research Centre ' Integrated Cities, Buildings & Components'

The information period has been closed off end 2006. The next phase is a one year long formation period containing the major research parties, the goals of the aimed synergetic collaboration, the common supply of research and development versus the demand from the different sections in the building industry and the resulting programming and collaborating Chairs.

Step 11: Mid term Review

The self studies are collected on 7 April; the site visit of the Mid Term Review is organized on 7 may 2007.

Step 12: Programming Building Technology Plus

The current programming could easily be joined with the respective researches on the TU Eindhoven and the research of the Buildings Department of Civil Engineering in order to attain an internationally stronger group of Dutch Building Technology. First collaborations are agreed already.

Step 13: Validation BT Plus

Also this new expanded program has to be validated like the validation described above in step 3.

Step 14: SME partnerships

In order to obtain and sound base of partnership with MKB /SME (small and medium business enterprises) different forms of partnerships and consortia will be exploited.

Step 15: Improving International Research Partnerships

In view of the attained research quality, but also in line with the expectations from FP 7 international research collaborations have to be initiated, exercised, entered and maintained.

Step 16: Tendering for the European 7 FP Program

On the base of large enough research groups (15 to 20 fte), international collaboration, international SME partnerships, tenders my be entered. This phase will be reached end of 2007 if all previous steps have been taken successively.

5.   Colloquia

Early 2007 the self studies of the programs were given (as per model of the official Qanu Assessments of the Dutch Universities: VS-NU). Followed by an overview per each of all relevant projects in the subprograms with a random sequence in which both the regular PhD students, the external PhD students, the staff researchers and guest researchers are represented. This overview had the form of a (standardized) poster in which ambitions, strategy results and a number of resulting or associated images are given. Each project is accompanied by a full page description, again according to an informative format per project of each researcher. At the end the epilogue gives a view on the future of these five Building Technology Research programs.

After a period of 3 years of growth and 1 year of clustering of individual research topics into consistent subprograms, the usual university validation time came. As is the rule in scientific research a selection was made of a number of internationally renown peers, whom we highly regard, are of independent stature and took the liberty to advise us their best views. We have invited the following peers:

- **Blobs**
  Prof.dr. Mannfred Grohmann Kassel
  Prof.dr. Branko Kolarevic Ball State University Indianapolis
  Prof.dr. Martin de Wit TU Eindhoven
- **Industrial Building**
  Prof.dr.Gerhard Hausladen Technische Universität München
  Prof.dr.Thomas Herzog Technische Universität München
  Prof. Richard Horden Technische Universität München
  Prof.dr.Jos Lichtenberg TU Eindhoven
  Prof.dr.Joop Halman UTwente
- **Informatics**
  Prof.dr.Robert Woodbury Universituy of Southern Maine
  Dr. Joop Paul Ove Arup NL
  Prof.dr. Imre Horvath Industrial Design Engineering TUDelft
- **Zappi**
  Prof.dr. Chris McMahon University of Bath
  Prof. Jan Vambersky, Civil Engineering TUDelft
  Prof.dr. Rob Nijsse University of Ghent, ABT, Arnhem
- **Climate Design**
  Prof.dr.Olaf Adan TU Eindhoven
  Prof.dr. Koen Steemers University of Cambridge
  Prof.dr. Frank de Troyer Katholieke Universteit Leuven

The peers have given their free and independent advice. Their advice is not contained in this lecture but bundled in a separate 'Internal Peer Review'. We received from them a critical analysis and further recommendations for the future of these research programs. They regarded the ongoing research in terms of newness, quality and validity. In total the 5 colloquia involved 17 international peers. This, in our opinion, was necessary as each aspect of technology has its own expertise and therefore requires the impulse from different technical aspects, more than the Mid Term Review Board, which will judge on a higher level of abstraction, is able to offer.

6. Development of this Research Program

The Assessment period for this Mid Term Review is 2003 – 2006. The first 3 years were used for expansion of the research, splitting up from the original 3 programs into the current 5 programs and internal cohesion of all programs. The last year was used in organizing the individual collection of research projects into coherent groupings. Via a number of organizational schemes in autumn 2006 the satellite schemes in 5 main programs and 15 subprograms resulted, see figure 2. In the last half year the scheme was hardly altered anymore. All researchers had to get accustomed with this arrangement, the strategic program leaders were appointed and the executive subprogram leaders were proposed, changed and finally appointed. They grew into their role. Of course 5 % of the researchers did not agree and continued to do their own, better way. They were right in the sense that this organizational set-up is artificial, because it is designed and could as well have been designed in another way. But this was the way of the research nestor. What is the right way? What is truth? It is an opinion, which may alter in time. But for the time being this organizational scheme, known as the Building Technology 'Orbit Scheme', is a recognizable set-up which researchers and outsiders understand easily. It is also a growth model. It does not make distinction between established and young researchers. On the contrary, it stimulates young researchers to become part of the existing group. It makes stepping in easier. The older researchers who do not see this growing need just continued their research, published their congress papers and did not mind. But gradually when the date of preparations came close, the recriminations, open and hidden, the debates and discussions became more intense. The idea of a scientific washing or colloquiums came from the assistant nestor Bige Tuncer. The colloquia meant an inevitable and historical step into the future. Each of the groups could choose 3 peers of their own liking, be it the most critical or the most compliant, depending how self-critical the peers were to be. By organizing peer reviewed colloquia an international standard was established, of which the results would be treated as historical data.

7. Peer Reviews

After the 5 colloquia have been organized, and at the moment of writing of this epilogue half of the peer reviews have been received, one could conclude that the peer review reports are quite diverse, That they contain 10 to 20% advised stops, 10 to 20% brilliant continuations and 60 to 80% advices for alterations of different degrees. All of them have to be collected and carefully analyzed and their advices followed up. As the complete Peer Review Collection took quite some time to be collected, the decision was taken to regard the (internal) peer reviews as being independent from the (external) Mid

Term Review. The peer review system is invented in order to get the best professionals from the research arena to give their best advices on the current research. There is no way back, no regrets and going back to individualism and only diving into one's own research. The reviews are a scientific phenomenon that has to be followed in order to become part of the international research community. The individual members of the Peer Review Boards all were highly esteemed peers in their specific profession. The Mid Term Review will no doubt advice on a more general level. Together they form the scientific evaluation of the research of Building Technology over the years 2003 to 2006.

8. Aim Of The Colloquia

One of the aims of organizing the colloquia was to force all researchers to speak themselves out to subject, mission, strategy and expected results. This alone caused quite some frictions between the supervisors and the researchers, which was to be expected. The research leaders became slowly aware that there was something to lead, a discipline to be enhanced, a common direction to be pursued, a future to be designed and to be developed. The steering upon a clearer direction and the debate on that only just began. Because the second aim was to communicate on one another's research amongst the researchers. Even the research program leaders obtained for the first time an overview over their research fields in the form of programs and only in the last weeks began to realize that a view on the future of their research program was expected from them in line of the obtained transparency.

9. The Building Technology - Projects Book

In the dazzling speed in which the preparations of the 5 colloquia had to be developed, the deadly consequence of one colloquium every 2 weeks took its toll on the side of the research nestor, assistant, layouters, editors and secretariat, all kind of small uprisings were common, but at the end all involved were satisfied with the result of these presentations. The results of the 5 colloquia were printed as the five BT Colloquium Books. This BT Projects Book can be regarded as the 6th volume, the final collection of all research projects which were underway at the marking date of 31 December 2006 or announced via vacancies. We know that the energy it took to get the scientific wheel rolling will be less on each occasion that an assessment or presentation is asked in future, or a publication is made. This research has been accepted by the individual researches.

The next 6 pages show 6 projects from the BT Projects Book that are part of the Façade Research Broup.

9.2.2 Systems in Façade Refurbishment

Ecologic and economic efficiency in "old" office buildings

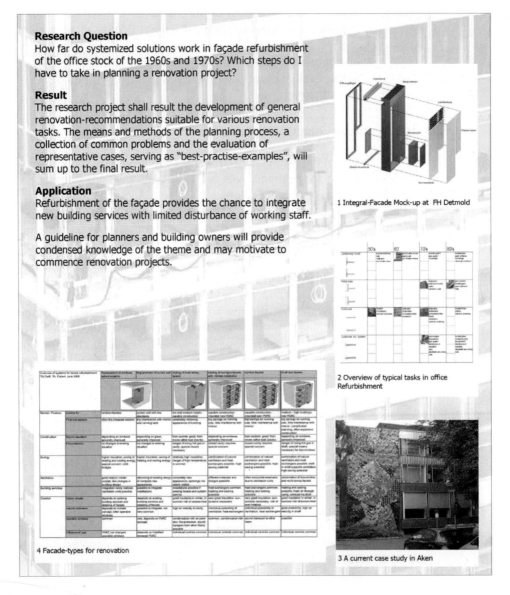

Research Question
How far do systemized solutions work in façade refurbishment of the office stock of the 1960s and 1970s? Which steps do I have to take in planning a renovation project?

Result
The research project shall result the development of general renovation-recommendations suitable for various renovation tasks. The means and methods of the planning process, a collection of common problems and the evaluation of representative cases, serving as "best-practise-examples", will sum up to the final result.

Application
Refurbishment of the façade provides the chance to integrate new building services with limited disturbance of working staff.

A guideline for planners and building owners will provide condensed knowledge of the theme and may motivate to commence renovation projects.

1 Integral-Facade Mock-up at FH Detmold

2 Overview of typical tasks in office Refurbishment

4 Facade-types for renovation

3 A current case study in Aken

Poster 9.2.2
Thiemo Ebbert

9.2.3 International façade

A PhD study on climate related façade constructions

Research Question
How and with which methods can one realise optimised façades that provide maximum comfort as well as economic efficiency in the facility operation for specific climate zones?

Result
The research project shall present an overview of façade requirements in different climate zones, useable as a guideline for architects and planners to increase the comfort and reduce the energy consumptions. In addition, new façade constructions shall be identified that exemplify improved adaptation to the regional climate than current projects. As a vision for the future new areas for research and development will be presented that provide potential for the development of façades.

traditional buildings, related to climate zone

current designs

moscow

china

Poster 9.2.3
Marcel Bilow

9.2.4 Integral Envelope

Towards Bionic Self-regulating Envelopes

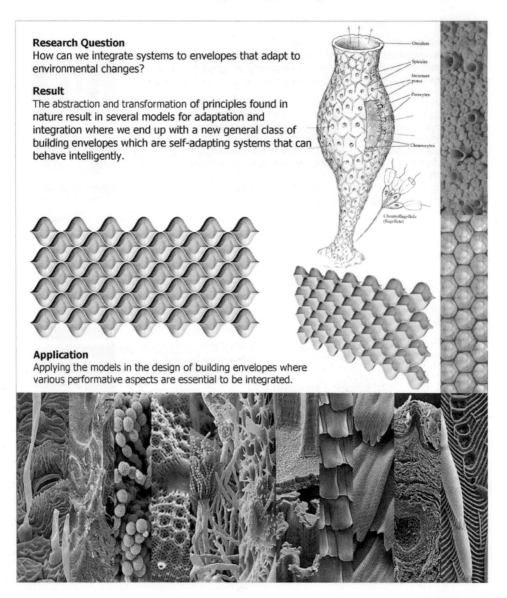

Research Question
How can we integrate systems to envelopes that adapt to environmental changes?

Result
The abstraction and transformation of principles found in nature result in several models for adaptation and integration where we end up with a new general class of building envelopes which are self-adapting systems that can behave intelligently.

Application
Applying the models in the design of building envelopes where various performative aspects are essential to be integrated.

Poster 9.2.4
Lida Badamah

9.2.5 Liquid Façade

Climate adaptive façade with liquid as regulating medium

Research question
How can liquid be used as a medium to vary the building physical properties of the façade, as a medium for building skin integrated heating and cooling and as collector of solar energy?

Result
Design of a climate adaptive façade with time, user and climate based (building physical) properties in which liquid is used as a medium to integrate the different technical solutions – shading, insulation, heating, etc. - within one materialization.

Application
New building skins for improving the energy performance of buildings.

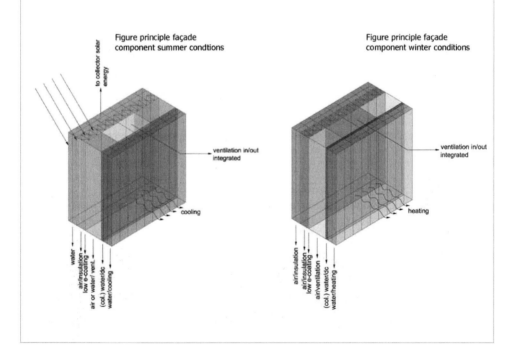

Poster 9.2.5
Arie Bergsma

9.2.6 Building a Visual Mockup Cleaning Robot

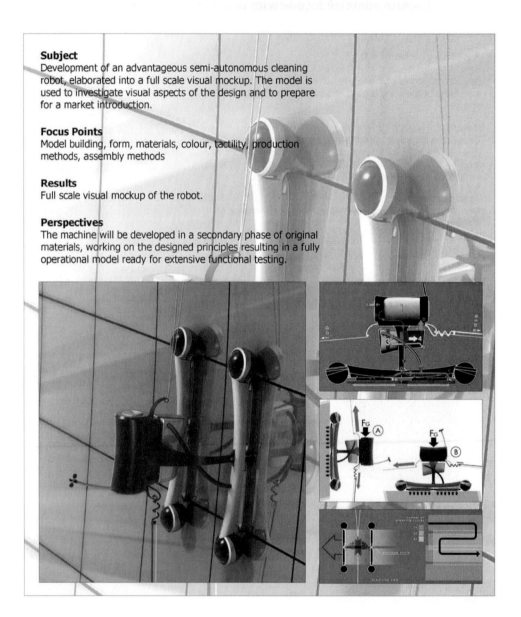

Subject
Development of an advantageous semi-autonomous cleaning robot, elaborated into a full scale visual mockup. The model is used to investigate visual aspects of the design and to prepare for a market introduction.

Focus Points
Model building, form, materials, colour, tactility, production methods, assembly methods

Results
Full scale visual mockup of the robot.

Perspectives
The machine will be developed in a secondary phase of original materials, working on the designed principles resulting in a fully operational model ready for extensive functional testing.

Poster 9.2.6
Maxim Eekhout

9.2.7 Technology Transfer

Integrated façade components

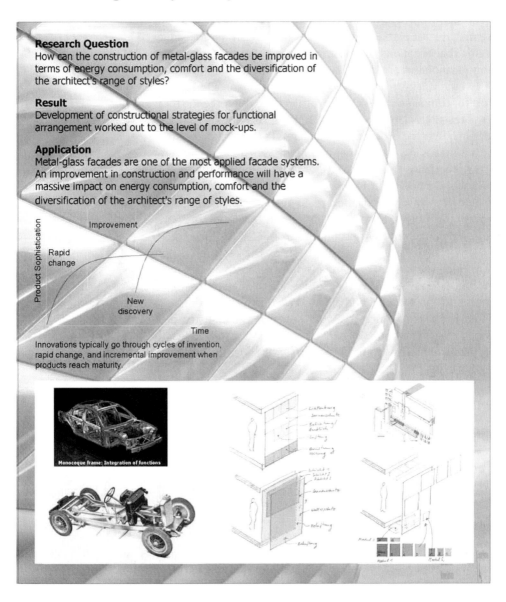

Research Question
How can the construction of metal-glass facades be improved in terms of energy consumption, comfort and the diversification of the architect's range of styles?

Result
Development of constructional strategies for functional arrangement worked out to the level of mock-ups.

Application
Metal-glass facades are one of the most applied facade systems. An improvement in construction and performance will have a massive impact on energy consumption, comfort and the diversification of the architect's range of styles.

Improvement

Rapid change

New discovery

Product Sophistication

Time

Innovations typically go through cycles of invention, rapid change, and incremental improvement when products reach maturity.

Monocoque frame: Integration of functions

Poster 9.2.7
Tillmann Klein

10.   Towards a 3TU Research Plan for Building Technology

The collection of all research projects described in this book, bundled in subprograms offers excellent possibilities for the following 2 steps in the near future: towards the tendering for the 7th Research Framework Program, FP7 (or in Dutch: KP7, '7e EU Kader Program) European subsidy programs, which in future will take over financing of research at least partially, a clustering of all scientific colleagues of specific specializations is almost mandatory. For that reason our Building Technology colleagues from TU Eindhoven and the University of Twente will be invited to join our programming and to make an effort for complimentary research projects, to reinforce the totality of the research plan into a Dutch Building Technology Research Plan. The minister has ordered the 3 Dutch TU's to collaborate. In research this means in a complementary mode. Since 7 February 2007 the 3TU Netherlands Federation is a fact. And although the top has set the pace, it is down to the shop floor, the faculty, to realize this adage. A logical reason to collaborate. Some of the professors from Eindhoven and Twente already collaborate in our programs (Lichtenberg, Halman) as do two professors from Civil Engineering TU Delft (Vambersky, Wagemans). Extension of the research potential from Eindhoven and Twente means more research power, more supervising manpower and more experience to share over the researchers and PhD students and more conviction towards the building industry to make alliances between research and industry, preferably nationally. This book will explain for the interested colleague researchers and players from the industry what quantity and quality they can expect.

11.   Quality Matters And Is Continously Strived For

Quantity has been expanded almost to the borders of what is possible to supervise. Also good PhD students are being attracted from other universities. Overseeing the result of the colloquia, quality on the average has still to grow. A number of the subprograms have only been initiated less than 2 years ago and are in their infancy, but the discipline and enthusiasm in the entire group will enable the younger research to lift along and learn from the elder researchers. This continuous process of eternal rejuvenation is common for PhD students operated research groups. The role of the research staff members is to supervise and to do their own long term research and to develop their vision on the future. This view on the future not only contains an extrapolation of the current situation, a scale-free expansion. But in future one should also try to find a match with the building industry in its four different parties that could be interested in the research results: clients/financers, architects/engineers, contractors/producers and planning/approving bodies. The match is mainly influenced by quality of the research. This valorisation finally fixes the value of scientific research for society, certainly in a faculty of Architecture which is proud to characterize itself as 'designing for society'.

12.   Research Centre 'Sp Bouw'

The next step, taken independently of the 3TU NL Federation is the initiative to form a Delft Research Centre for Building, which has the working title "Integrated Cities, Buildings & Components". In this research centre all related research would be concentrated from the 3 Delft faculties of Architecture, Civil Engineering and Technology, Policy & Management plus the TU Delft OTB Institute in first instance, later to be followed by the respective researchers from Eindhoven and Twente into a National Research Centre. In this research centre the three levels of Cities / Infrastructure, Buildings / Structures and Components / Materials are distinguished. The three levels will contain 8 or 9 different research groups of each 3 to 4 research chairs in integrated collaboration, in size manageable. But at the same time as a totality transparent in its strategy of deduction from societal problems via technical problems and building technical problems to the research questions of the respective groups. In order to enhance the societal factor of interest in the research one could think on several societal problems which need attention, for example: Increasing Mobility, Decreasing Population, Expected Greying, Enhanced Informatization, Energy Consumption, Intensive Urbanism, Further Industrialization and Rising Water Levels / Sinking Bottoms. In view of validation all research projects contribute towards trying to solve partially these societal problems. Of course there will be specific Chair research to keep the level of knowledge in the Chair sharp, but these will be separated from the integral approach contained in the research centre described. This global research plan for the Building Industry in the Netherlands will no doubt get to know its open or convert agnostics and adversaries, but it is worth while stepping into this adventure of a nation-wide research plan for the building industry, which internationally does not make a lively and fresh impression and could use an injection of new know-how and insight.

13.   Enlarging the Research Plan In 2007

The year 2007 time will be taken to form this research plan in consultation with the respective researchers (supply side) and the respective players form the building industry (demand). Only when this match between demand and supply matures, the new plan will be put into operation. If the match will not mature, the future research will be maintained on the level of the different departments, like the research plan of Building Technology enriched by the 3TU Thinking.

It is our goal to start discussions with the colleagues of the other 3 departments to see whether they share our vision and want to enter into a similar organization, with the result that they would participate in the new research program as described above.

14.   Match between Demand and Supply

In this case of a revolutionary new approach involving the demand side, the current integrated set-up of our research plan will probably hinder a renovation. So the renovation will be prepared by concentrating all research into chair research plans, which are grouped again and integrated into the very topics that seems applicable for the demand side of the building industry or / and from society. There could be a danger involved with such a close match in collaboration with the demand side, which is their capriciousness. Research will focus on the long run of at least 6 to 12 years, in academic 6-year cycles of the assessments. That means that even researchers have to focus both on a medium term goal of 6 years and on a long term goal of 12 years, while industries may appear and disappear in the meantime. Also researchers start and complete and professors are inaugurated and retire. But these are the cycles a sturdy program must be able to survive. The program goes beyond the issues of the day or the hobbies of the professor in charge. The program should be well-written for the non-specialist, transparent, convincing and directed towards a long duration with intervals of results in output of whatever kind (reports, prototypes, testing, designs) in its collaborations. A clear and specific program will obtains its financing thereafter.

15. Conclusions for Façades

This article contains an elaborate treatise of how our research has been set up, how the peer reviews were prepared in research colloquia and how the future of this research will be organized. We have a fair trust in the force behind this set-up, which enables our professors to be centres of the research subject and enable parties from the outside; international scientists as well as national and international façade industry to participate in this future 'Integrated Façade' TU Delft research group which will come out of these considerations within a few months. The posters of the respective sub-programs of 'Skins' and 'Comfort' were deliberately not yet included as the discussions with these researchers only have begun. But indications can be derived from figure 3. The 'Future Integrated Façade' has a core of research with which other universities in Europe and the research & development departments of the larger façade industries are invited to join in and participate in this development in the coming 7 to 8 years. Around this core of research prof. Knaack wraps his International Façade Master, so that a research driven education will support this research as well.

At the first Blobs Colloquium on 25 January 2007 dr. Wim Poelman presented, at request from the audience, 8 poems written by Paulo Coelho from his book 'Manual of the Warrior of Light' (ISBN 0 00 715632 4), which illuminate the start and the end of this contribution and illustrate the research atmosphere.

> Before embarking on an important battle, a warrior of light asks himself: 'How far have I developed my abilities?'
>
> He knows that he has learned something with every battle he has fought, but many of those lessons have caused him unnecessary suffering. More than once he has wasted his time fighting for a lie. And he has suffered for people who did not deserve his love.
>
> Victors never make the mistake twice. That is why the warrior only risks his heart for something worthwhile.

Prof.dr.Mick Eekhout,
Research Nestor Building Technology

References

1   Just Renckens, 'Aluminium Facades & Architecture' , TUDelft / VM-RG / VAS / FAECF, 1996, ISBN, 3-00-002321-6 (available at secretariat Building technology TU Delft;

2   Michael Chrisnel, Mick Eekhout, Matthias Haldemann, Ronald Visser, 'EU COST 13 Final report Glass & Interactive Building Envelopes' , IOS Press, , Amsterdam, 2006, ISBN 978-1-58603-709-3

3   Sevil Sariyildiz, Mick Eekhout, Paula van den Bergh, Meerjarenplan Afdeling Bouwtechnologie 2006-2009, Internal publication, secretariat Building Technology TU Delft

4   Mick Eekhout, Ronald Visser et al, 'Research Colloquium Industrial Building, 8 February 2007' Department of Building Technology

5   Mick Eekhout, Ronald Visser et al, 'Building technology research projects 31 december 2006' Department of Building Technology TU Delft

Naturally, we also used this conference to evaluate and readjust our own research – the multidisciplinary approach delivers a broad range of influences and opportunities that need to be organised and directed meaningfully: the roadmap drawn from the conclusion of the conference.

The Future Envelope 1 – A Multidisciplinary Approach. U. Knaack and T. Klein (Eds.). IOS Press, 2008.

ROADMAP FOR THE FUTURE ENVELOPE

Ulrich Knaack
Tillmann Klein

As a research institution we have to develop visions for the future in order to guide our efforts in an appropriate and meaningful direction. But how can we create a vision that stands up for the next 5, 10, or better yet, 20 years for a discipline, which is based on a long tradition and involves a great number of technologies?

The idea was born to invite specialists from our own and other disciplines to compare and share ideas. These specialists were asked to talk about their particular work and experiences, and to share their vision for the future.

The symposium „The Future Envelope" was held on June 11th, 2007 at the TU Delft / Faculty of Architecture and as the head of the chair we would like to outline a brief roadmap for possible developments for enveloping facades and structures. The conclusion is based on the papers and opinion of the speakers, as well as the discussions with the auditorium during the conference. It sums up the demands for future research investigation, possible themes and strategies.

Current Status of the Metal-Glass Facade

As a starting point for future strategies, we are looking at the current status of state-of-the-art post-and-rail constructions, the element-facades. They are well known and commonly used. The underlying principle has not changed over the last 50 years; its main aspects have undergone extensive research and investigation. This fact is proven by, for example, only marginal improvements in terms of energy performance.

The Next Step: Integrated Facades and Comfort Industry

Integration was one of the most frequently used terms of the conference, related to the different levels of the process of facade construction. The philosophy of integration begins in the planning phase and ends with the physical components.

Two areas were specifically identified: the construction and building services. Both areas will need more integrated planning in the future to fulfil the demands on the future envelope.

Climate control is another important area of façade design that requires an integrated planning approach. Ideas described during the conference combined various service units into element facades, which, in some cases, could be double facades.

The difficulties become obvious when we think about the planning and construction processes – the integration process itself during planning, where the disciplines not only have to communicate well and continuously, but also have to use the same data model; and during production and assembly, where, not only organizational issues have to be solved, but also the difficulty of who assumes liability for the final product.

Several companies currently work along this trend; with one company typically assuming the leading role (usually a systems provider) and building services components being added to the system. Examples herefor are the products T-motion by Hydro Building Systems and the Schüco e² Facade.

An alternative to this concept could be a collaborative development. Companies from different disciplines form a long-term partnership with the goal to develop integrated components or entire facade systems. VMRG (Vereniging Metalen Ramen en Gevelbranche) announced to take the stakeholder position in developing combined enterprises within the Dutch façade and services industry.

This step offers a new perspective. Action is not only taken on a project by project basis and in a directly value orientated manner, but aims for strategic development and therefore opens up opportunities for innovation.

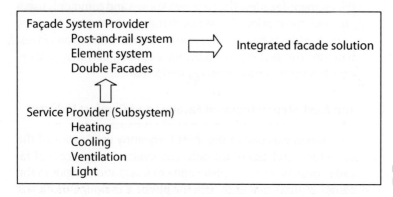

Figure 1
Integrated Façade Solutions

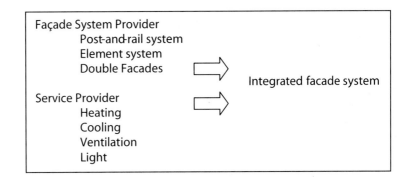

Figure 2
Collaborative Approach

The Strategic Development: Performance Oriented Envelopes

Asking speakers from not building oriented disciplines for their input provides new perspectives for strategies, influences

and impulses for alternative, even unexpected and new directions. This was the case when asking aeronautic

engineers and product developers for there visions. One result of this input was that the perspective of façade research has to change. Innovations typically go through cycles of invention, rapid change, and incremental improvement when products reach maturity. Related to the façade, research in the development of existing systems must look into the functionality requirements of the future envelope. We have to define the demands in the fields of construction and climate control, but also consider aesthetic and formal aspects.

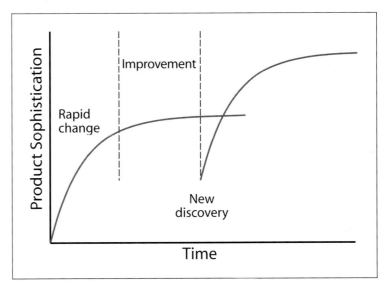

Figure 3
Innovations typically go through cycles of invention, rapid change, and incre-mental improvement when products reach maturity.

The design of goal should be the focus, not the design of means (Wim Poelman). In the past, solution oriented thinking, based on existing construction methods, has lead to simply layering more and more functions, therefore increasing complexity.

However, we need to concentrate on ways, where the soılution is developed and constructed out of the request:

The performance oriented envelope.

The strategy for this idea would be to conduct research in the specific user request and the demands of the building (functionalities). The next step is to investigate technologies that will support the results of the request and, if they are not available, find them in another discipline, using the methodology of technology transfer.

We do not only have to play the role of a generalist, but more of an integralist with the capability to create the interface between different fields.

Proposals made during the conference for the performance oriented façade were called adaptable facades or pliable facades – facades that can react to various climate and lighting conditions as well as individual user requirements. These facades have to be able to change there performance during the course of the day and the different climate periods of the year. At the same time, they could be developed for other geographic and climatic regions, were they do not have to change during the time of use.

Technical solutions for this proposal guide us to composite materials and generic production methods such as rapid manufacturing: the requirement of a combination of different functions will lead to a non-element result, were the system provides the principle of combination but not a defined number of possibilities. Depending on the request from the users and the demands of the building, the envelope has to be combined and produced for unique situations and unique results – also from an aesthetic point of view.

To investigate technical solutions and possible developments, the façade research group will continue with there instrument "Future Facade Principles" which is a collection of façade and envelope technologies, developed without immediate aesthetic or architectural solutions in mind, but to find inspiration for new designs.

Personal Conclusions of the Conference

Besides the above mentioned aspects for the roadmap of the development of the future envelope, the chairmen of the conference would like to draw some personal conclusions for the future:

We have to take responsibility! Innovation can be provoked by breaking out off established patterns. Various examples of inspiring projects, developments and detail solutions were shown and explained. One common criterion of all these examples was that the designers and manufacturers all took a personal risk to arrive at the final solution. Without this attitude and by always remaining within the explicitly allowed regulations, the development of mankind as we know it today would not have taken place.

We also have to conclude that in addition to the fruitful discussions, more controversial communication needs to take place. An example: the idea of facades integration first and performance orientation second, was, of course, a result of the conference; however, the discussion about mass customization versus individuality shows, that people still have very different views of what the correct solution should be. Mass customization with its new possibilities by using CAD / CAM is required to solve the difficulties of individual solutions for systemized constructions. Contrary though, the idea of individual solutions, obviously extremely established in architecture, demands maximum object oriented solutions. Presumably, this conflict can never be solved – maybe the solution is to define the amount of individual and systemized components for each project individually– which in itself is an object oriented solution.

Luke Lowings found the right words: "The aspiration is to move towards a mature resolution of our relationship to our context, not just the dry level of efficiency and the use of resources, but emotionally, symbolically and perceptually."

In closing, we would like to thank all participants (lecturers and audience), the industry (represented by VMRG), and conclude with the last part of Michiel Cohen´s text: "The future should be more simple". It is up to us to find ways to achieve this in spite of increasing complexity.